T0318166

A Computational Model of Industry Dynamics

The economics literature on industry dynamics contains a wide array of empirical works identifying a set of stylized facts. There have been several attempts at constructing analytical models to explain some of these regularities. These attempts are highly stylized and limited in scope to keep the analyses tractable. A general model of industry evolution capable of generating firm and industry behavior that can match the data is needed.

This book endeavors to explain many well-documented aspects of the evolution of industries over time. It uses an agent-based computational model in which artificial industries are created and grown to maturity *in silico*. While the firms in the model are assumed to have bounded rationality, they are nevertheless adaptive in the sense that their experience-based R&D efforts allow them to search for improved technologies. Given a technological environment subject to persistent and unexpected external shocks, the computationally generated industry remains in a perennial state of flux. The main objective of this study is to identify patterns that exist in the movements of firms as the industry evolves over time along the steady state in which the measured behavior of the firms and the industry stochastically fluctuate around steady means.

The computational model developed in this book is able to replicate many of the stylized facts from the empirical industrial organization literature, particularly as the facts pertain to the dynamics of firm entry and exit. Furthermore, the model allows examination of cross-industry variations in entry and exit patterns by systematically varying the characteristics of the market and the technological environment within which the computationally generated industry evolves. The model demonstrates that the computational approach based on boundedly rational agents in a dynamic setting can be useful and effective in carrying out both positive and normative economic analysis.

Myong-Hun Chang is Professor and Chair of the Department of Economics, Cleveland State University, USA.

Routledge Advances in Experimental and Computable Economics
Edited by K. Vela Velupillai and
Stefano Zambelli, *University of Trento, Italy*

1. **The Economics of Search**
   Brian and John McCall

2. **Classical Econophysics**
   Paul Cockshott et al.

3. **The Social Epistemology of Experimental Economics**
   Ana Cordeiro dos Santos

4. **Computable Foundations for Economics**
   K. Vela Velupillai

5. **Neuroscience and the Economics of Decision Making**
   Edited by Alessandro Innocenti and Angela Sirigu

6. **Computational Intelligence Techniques for Trading and Investment**
   Edited by Christian Dunis, Spiros Likothanassis, Andreas Karathanasopoulos, Georgios Sermpinis and Konstantinos Theofilatos

7. **A Computational Model of Industry Dynamics**
   Myong-Hun Chang

Other books in the Series include:

Economics Lab
An intensive course in experimental economics
Alessandra Cassar and Dan Friedman

A Computational Model of Industry Dynamics

Myong-Hun Chang

Routledge
Taylor & Francis Group

LONDON AND NEW YORK

First published 2015 by Routledge

2 Park Square, Milton Park, Abingdon, Oxfordshire OX14 4RN
52 Vanderbilt Avenue, New York, NY 10017

Routledge is an imprint of the Taylor & Francis Group, an informa business

First issued in paperback 2020

Copyright © 2015 Myong-Hun Chang

The right of Myong-Hun Chang to be identified as author of this work has been asserted in accordance with sections 77 and 78 of the Copyright, Designs and Patent Act 1988.

All rights reserved. No part of this book may be reprinted or reproduced or utilised in any form or by any electronic, mechanical, or other means, now known or hereafter invented, including photocopying and recording, or in any information storage or retrieval system, without permission in writing from the publishers.

Notice:
Product or corporate names may be trademarks or registered trademarks, and are used only for identification and explanation without intent to infringe.

British Library Cataloguing in Publication Data
A catalogue record for this book is available from the British Library

Library of Congress Cataloguing in Publication data
A catalog record for this book has been requested.

ISBN: 978-0-415-70684-1 (hbk)
ISBN: 978-0-367-59981-2 (pbk)

Typeset in Times New Roman
by Out of House Publishing

To the memory of my father

"[T]he central idea of economics, even when its Foundations alone are under discussion, must be that of living force and movement."
Principles of Economics, Alfred Marshall

Contents

List of figures   ix
List of tables   xii
Preface   xiii
Acknowledgments   xv

1   **Non-equilibrium dynamics in the evolution of industries**   1
     Notes 8

2   **Models of industry dynamics**   9
     2.1 Stationary equilibrium models and the purely analytical approach 10
     2.2 Markov perfect equilibrium models and the computational approach 11
     2.3 Agent-based computational economics approach 12
     Notes 15

3   **A dynamic model of Schumpeterian competition**   17
     3.1 Conceptual building blocks 17
     3.2 The model: basic features 22
     3.3 The model: dynamic structure 28
     Notes 40

4   **Growing an industry *in silico***   42
     4.1 Design of computational experiments 42
     4.2 The baseline: generating the proto-history 47
     Notes 53

5   **Shakeouts: limited foresight, technological shocks, and
    transient industry dynamics**   54
    5.1   Shakeout in an infant industry 58
    5.2   Technological change and recurrent shakeouts 71
        Notes 75

6   **Industry dynamics in the steady state: between-
    industry variations**   76
    6.1   Defining the steady state 77
    *6.2   Temporal patterns along the steady state within
          an industry 79*
    6.3   Between-industry variations in steady states 84
    6.4   Implications for cross-industries studies 95
        Notes 97

7   **Firm dynamics in the steady state: within-industry
    variations**   99
    7.1   Technological diversity 99
    7.2   Market share inequality 104
    7.3   Life span of firms 106

8   **Cyclical industrial dynamics with fluctuating demand**   115
    8.1   An overview 117
    8.2   Stochastic variation in demand 120
    8.3   Deterministic variation in demand 123
    8.4   Summary 129
        Notes 130

9   **Conclusion**   131

References   135
Index   140

Figures

3.1 Four stages of decision making by firms in
     period t 30
3.2 Sequence of R&D decisions within stage 2   36
4.1 Time series of endogenous turnovers from a single
     replication   48
4.2 Mean time series of endogenous turnovers from
     500 independent replications   49
4.3 Mean time series of endogenous performance
     variables from 500 independent replications   51
4.4 Time series of technological diversity and market
     share inequality (Gini coefficient)   52
5.1 Number of producers in US automobile industry
     between 1895 and 1966   56
5.2 Entries and exits in US automobile industry
     between 1895 and 1966   56
5.3 Proportion of firms exiting the US automobile
     industry between 1895 and 1966 that were of a
     given age (AGE) or younger   57
5.4 Turnover in US automobile tire industry   59
5.5 Baseline computational results from a single
     replication over the Jovanovic-MacDonald time span   60
5.6 Mean time series of endogenous variables from
     500 independent replications   62
5.7 Mean time series of technological diversity and
     market share inequality from 500 independent replications   63
5.8 Impact of fixed cost (f) on shakeout   64
5.9 Impact of fixed cost (f) on shakeout   65
5.10 Impact of fixed cost (f) on shakeout   66

5.11   Impact of market size (s) on shakeout   67
5.12   Impact of market size (s) on shakeout   69
5.13   Impact of market size (s) on shakeout   70
5.14   Frequency of various durations of episodes from
     a single replication   72
5.15   Duration of episodes and the size of firm
     movements   72
5.16   Relationship between the endogenous variables
     and the time since the last technological shift   73
5.17   Relationship between the endogenous variables
     and the time since the last technological shift   74
6.1   Average rate of entry and average rate of exit
     across 20 two-digit sectors   77
6.2   Impact of market size (s) and fixed cost (f) on firm
     turnover   86
6.3   Impact of market size (s) and fixed cost (f) on
     intra-industry volatility (frequency of leadership changes)   87
6.4   Histograms from the 500 independent
     replications, with and without endogenous R&D   89
6.5   Impact of market size (s) and fixed cost (f) on
     R&D   91
6.6   Impact of market size (s) and fixed cost (f) on
     industry structure   92
6.7   Impact of market size (s) and fixed cost (f) on
     industry performance   94
7.1   Steady-state mean technological diversity:
     histograms from the 500 independent replications,
     with and without endogenous R&D   101
7.2   Impact of R&D costs, K_{IN} and K_{IM} 102
7.3   Impact of market size (s) and fixed cost (f) on the
     steady-state mean technological diversity   103
7.4   Steady-state mean market share inequality:
     histograms from the 500 independent replications,
     with and without endogenous R&D   105
7.5   Impact of R&D costs, K_{IN} and K_{IM}, on steady-
     state mean market share inequality   105
7.6   Impact of market size (s) and fixed cost (f) on the
     steady-state mean market share inequality   106

7.7	Distribution of ages of exiting firms in the US auto industry (1895–1966)	107
7.8	Best fit for the distribution of ages of exiting firms in the US auto industry (1895–1966)	108
7.9	Distribution of ages of exiting firms from the computational model (bin size = 1)	109
7.10	Distribution of ages of exiting firms from the computational model (bin size = 200)	110
7.11	Best fit for the distribution of ages of exiting firms from the computational model (bin size = 200)	111
7.12	Impact of endogenous R&D on the distribution of ages of exiting firms from the computational model (bin size = 200)	112
7.13	Proportion of firms exiting the industry that were of a given age (AGE) or younger	113
8.1	Industry dynamics when market size is stochastic	121
8.2	Deterministic demand cycle	124
8.3	Cyclical dynamics of market price and industry profits	125
8.4	Cyclical dynamics of industry structure	126
8.5	Cyclical dynamics of industry performance	127
8.6	Cyclical dynamics of industry marginal cost with and without endogenous R&D	128
8.7	Cyclical dynamics of aggregate R&D spending	129

Tables

3.1	Set notations	31
3.2	Beliefs underlying the firms' decision-making	32
3.3	Evolving attractions	39
4.1	List of parameters and their values	43
6.1	Steady-state means of the endogenous variables	78
6.2	Correlations between endogenous variables	80
6.3	Relationships between the industry-specific factors and the endogenous variables	96
7.1	Fitted value of the exponent for the power law ($\hat{a}$)	112
8.1	Correlations between the market size and the endogenous variables	122
8.2	Cyclicality of the endogenous variables	130

Preface

The computational model of industry dynamics presented in this book evolved out of several generations of earlier primitive versions that went through the usual process of natural and artificial selection in the academic setting. The very first version focused solely on the shakeout dynamics in an infant industry with no external technological shocks. The results from this preliminary version were reported in an article published in the *Journal of Economic Interactions and Coordination* (2009). The second version allowed for external technological shocks but with no adaptive R&D by the firms. The results from this model were reported in a chapter in *Oxford Handbook of Computational Economics and Finance* (forthcoming). The third version of the model with exogenously specified R&D by firms was presented in *Eastern Economic Journal* (2011).

The most general version of this line of models is reported in this book and allows firms to adapt to external technological shocks by autonomously performing R&D in search of improved technologies. Making the process of R&D endogenous has enabled a re-examination of the issues explored in the earlier publications under richer market and technological conditions. More importantly, it has created the ability to address a new set of questions that are unique to Schumpeterian competition with innovative and imitative R&D.

I have two goals in this book. The first is to model a set of well-known stylized facts in empirical Industrial Organization, involving entries and exits of firms over time. While various attempts have been made to understand these patterns as part of the "industry equilibrium" in the context of profit-maximizing firms with perfect foresight, the scale and scope of investigations have been rather limited due to either the restrictive nature of the assumptions used to foster tractability, or the formidable analytical difficulties resulting from less restrictive assumptions. The computational model developed here eschews the standard behavioral assumptions in the tradition of "orthodox" economic theory. Instead, the dynamic patterns arising at the level of an industry are viewed as the result of continuing interactions among myopic and heterogeneous firms which are motivated by profit and engaged in R&D as a way to improve their profits. The ultimate objective is then to understand the stylized facts as patterns that arise endogenously as firms make adaptive moves against unexpected external shocks as well as to each other in their search for improved profits.

The second, more general, goal of the book is to explore and demonstrate the capability of computational modeling in making theoretical advances in those areas of economics traditionally thought to be the exclusive domain of analytical methodology based on equilibrium theorizing. As I hope to show in the following chapters, questions not easily answered using orthodox equilibrium models can be resolved and examined in some detail within a computational model of boundedly rational agents.

Although the present study does not go further than to offer positive analyses for explanatory purposes, the further challenge for the approach will be the extent of its capacity to offer normative prescription through policy experiments performed on a platform sophisticated enough to capture the finer details of the real industries. I hope to have made a preliminary contribution to this endeavor by writing this book.

Acknowledgments

The research reported in this book was presented at several national and international conferences: 2010 International Industrial Organization Conference (Vancouver); 2010 International Computational Economics & Finance Conference (London); 2011 International Industrial Organization Conference (Boston); 2012 Eastern Economic Association Conference (Boston); 2012 Workshop on Economic Heterogeneous Interacting Agents (Paris); 2012 International Computational Economics & Finance Conference (Prague); 2013 Eastern Economic Association Conference (New York). I have benefitted from the comments and suggestions of the session participants from these conferences. In particular, I would like to thank Jason Barr, Johannes Koenen, Chris Ruebeck, and Robert Somogyi for their detailed comments.

At the home front, I have received helpful comments and assistance from a number of colleagues both while working on the model and on various drafts of this book; I am especially grateful to Ed Bell, Jon Harford, and Doug Stewart for many stimulating conversations that proved valuable in refining the model presented here. Both Jon Harford and Doug Stewart made useful editorial comments on earlier drafts of the manuscript. In particular, Jon was gracious enough to read the manuscript in its entirety and offer invaluable advice. I have incorporated the substance of nearly all of his suggestions in my text.

I have also been assisted by a number of capable graduate assistants over the years. Although not included in this book, Amanda Janosco carried out the data collection effort for the study of firm turnovers in the East Liverpool (Ohio) pottery industry, which substantially improved my understanding of the entry and exit process. Charlotte DeKoning, Endrit Meta, and Chris Cox provided editorial assistance at various stages of the writing process. Endrit deserves special thanks for transforming the entry/exit data from the US auto industry (Smith (1968)) into a manageable dataset as visualized in Chapter 5.

I am pleased to acknowledge the institutional support I received from Cleveland State University during the project. I was granted a sabbatical leave in the spring of 2009 to work on the initial development of the project. Dean Greg Sadlek of the College of Liberal Arts and Social Sciences allowed release time during the summer of 2014 to complete the manuscript. Finally, this research was partially funded by the Faculty Research Development Grant (0210-0382-10) from the College of Graduate Studies at Cleveland State University. The groundwork was laid during the grant period of 2008–2011. This book is the final product.

1 Non-equilibrium dynamics in the evolution of industries

The evolution of market structure is a complex phenomenon and the quest for any single model that encompasses all the statistical regularities observed is probably not an appropriate goal. Yet there remain phenomena which may well be worth encompassing in a more general theory than is currently available, and which are still poorly understood. Most notable among these are questions of the industry-specific determinants of firm turnover (turbulence) and the volatility of market shares. Another such area is that of the pattern of exit in declining industries. Notwithstanding recent progress on these topics, many important questions still remain open.

[Sutton (1997), p. 57]

This research was motivated by four stylized facts in empirical Industrial Organization (IO). The first is the phenomenon of shake-out in infant industries. This widely reported phenomenon describes the sudden inflow of firms at the birth of an industry, followed by a rapid outflow of firms that bears a striking resemblance to a market crash. This is a phenomenon that has been documented extensively.[1] The second is the observation that the entries and exits of firms persist in the long run even in mature industries. Third, the movements into and out of the industry tend to occur together when they occur: a period of high rate of entry is also the one of a high rate of exit. Finally, the severity of such structural turbulence tends to differ across industries. Some industries are characterized by high rates of entry and exit, while others are characterized by relatively low rates of entry and exit. This calls for a systematic study of how the shape, size, and nature of the industry dynamics are determined by the industry-specific factors:[2]

A last observation concerns the enormous variation across new industries in the pace and severity of the prototypical pattern of industry evolution. This suggests that there are important differences across industries in the factors that condition the evolutionary process.

[Klepper and Graddy (1990), p. 37]

[W]e find substantial and persistent differences in entry and exit rates across industries. Entry and exit rates at a point in time are also highly correlated across industries, so that industries with higher than average entry rates tend to also have higher than average exit rates. Together these suggest that industry-specific factors play an important role in determining entry and exit patterns.

[Dunne et al. (1988), p. 496]

It was with the belief that any credible model of industrial dynamics must account for these phenomena that I embarked on the search for a comprehensive model of industry competition. I further believed such a model should be capable of making predictions on the long-run structure and performance of an industry that are consistent with the empirical evidence accumulated over many years in the standard IO literature. What emerged out of this search is the general model of industry dynamics that I present here. This general model allows one to perform a wide variety of computational experiments, successfully replicate the stylized facts mentioned above, and make additional predictions based on the underlying theory of firm behavior and market competition.

The model presented here is motivated by a couple of initial impressions on what may constitute the causal mechanism driving the dynamics of firms and industries. First, the dramatic rise and fall in the number of firms during a shakeout suggests a degree of myopia on the part of entrants. Second, business firms grapple with unexpected shocks to their operating environment on a daily basis – shocks that create new profit opportunities for some but simultaneously drive others to extinction. Such non-uniform effects of unanticipated external shocks can induce correlations between the entry and exit rates of firms across time (i.e., a period with an above-average rate of entry also has an above-average rate of exit) and across industries (i.e., the industry with an above-average rate of entry also has an above-average rate of exit).

More formally, the proposed model has four features that I believe are important for generating and understanding the stylized facts:

a) *Bounded rationality*: Each firm has limited foresight and is unable to form "rational expectation" as typically assumed in the economics literature.

b) *Variation in technologies*: There are different methods (technologies) for producing the same good. When firms in an industry employ different technologies, they may realize different levels of production efficiency.

c) *Persistent technological shocks*: Firms are constantly subjected to unexpected shocks in their technological environment; these shocks directly and asymmetrically affect their production efficiency and the likelihood of survival from market competition. In this context, I use the term "asymmetrically" to indicate the fact that some firms benefit from the shocks while others are adversely affected by them. The shocks are assumed to be caused by inventions and innovations that originate from outside the industry and affect all firms in the industry.

d) *R&D as adaptive search*: Firms adapt to the changing technological environment by investing in R&D that may improve their production efficiency through the process of search for a technology better suited for the new environment.

The standard approach in mainstream economic theory is to assume full rationality and, by implication, unlimited cognitive capability on the part of decision makers. There are two well-known arguments that have been presented in defense of this assumption (Friedman (1953)). The first is the argument that the decision maker, even if he does not consciously behave in the way described by the procedure of perfectly rational choice, can be viewed as behaving *as if* he follows such a procedure. The second argument rests on an evolutionary explanation, in which the firms behaving according to the maximization hypothesis – consistent with full rationality assumption – have a better chance of survival in the competitive market arena and come to dominate over time through the process of natural selection.

The decision making criteria used by firms in the model presented here depart significantly from those employed in the standard mainstream literature. Instead of assuming perfect rationality, I assume a substantial degree of "bounded rationality" in several important aspects of the firms' decision making process. First, all firms are myopic; they make their decisions on the basis of the static single-period profits rather than the present value of the stream of discounted expected profits as typically assumed. Second, the static single-period profits used for firms' decision making are informed by the actual *realized* state of the market from the previous period and not by the *expected* state of the market that takes into account the anticipated moves of other firms in the current period. Hence, there is no "perfect foresight" in this model. Instead, firms are backward-looking but adaptive in their decision making in that their decisions are consistently made on the basis of the *lagged* information from the previously observed state of the market.

These features of bounded rationality imply a rather special set of decision criteria for the firms in the model. First, the market that a potential entrant envisions upon entry is the one he observed prior to his entry with himself as the only additional player. Second, a potential entrant contemplating entry into the market bases its decision on the single period profit he would earn upon entry.

The backward-looking (or recent-history-based) behavior also extends to the R&D investment behavior of the incumbent firms in this model. The choices of whether or not to invest in R&D and what type of R&D (i.e., innovative vs. imitative R&D) to pursue are made probabilistically, where the choice probabilities evolve over time according to how each strategy performed relative to other available strategies in the past. It is, hence, the past experience of a firm that guides its R&D decisions; not the payoff expectation computed on the basis of all possible future states of the world. To the extent that the choice probabilities are updated on the basis of the most recent experience, this mechanism reflects the *adaptive* nature in the behavior of firms.

There are two reasons, one conceptual and the other practical, why the use of bounded rationality is deemed appropriate in this research. The first reason is that the central issue under investigation deals with market conditions that are highly stochastic and thus lead to inherently turbulent market structure. In the context of our model, these market conditions include the following: 1) the technological environment is subject to continual external shocks which affect the efficiencies of the operating firms randomly across time and asymmetrically across firms; and 2) firms with heterogeneous technologies enter and exit the market each period, thus inducing persistent volatility in the structure of the market. These factors lead to a decision environment that is fraught with uncertainty and incomplete information. In this environment a rational pursuit of expected profit maximization is made difficult by the limited ability of a decision maker to predict the inter-temporal movements of the variables that determine the future states,[3] and it is appropriate to make the assumption of bounded rationality.

The second reason for limiting the degree of rationality is more practical. As modeled here, firms with bounded rationality use fixed decision rules. Fixed decision rules substantially reduce the demand for computational resources required in the dynamic optimization process. In the present context, one in which a large number of firms with heterogeneous technologies engage in market interactions while facing a technological environment subject to persistent random shocks, the consequence of assuming perfect rationality is that each firm must solve a stochastic dynamic programming problem in which all possible future states of its rivals conditional on those shocks are fully incorporated (given that the firm holds well-defined subjective beliefs over these shocks and these beliefs are common knowledge to all firms in the market). This process presents a computational problem of significant complexity, and it is difficult, if not impossible, for the modeler to keep the model sufficiently rich in detail to generate predictions that can fit the observed data while retaining its analytical tractability. Even the "numerical" methods intended to avoid the very issue of tractability (while remaining in the dynamic optimization framework) suffer from the "curse of dimensionality" which comes with the exponential growth in the size of the state space resulting from the increase in the number of variables. In other words, the computational cost of solving the dynamic programming problems with multiple players (firms), each with multiple choice variables, quickly becomes prohibitive. The use of fixed decision rules, by passing over the dynamic optimization process, allows computational resources to be reallocated to tracking and analyzing the adaptive behavior of a realistically large number of firms as they interact with one another over time as the industry grows to its maturity.

The remaining three features of the model, (b) through (d), provide the conceptual basis for understanding industry dynamics as a manifestation of an evolutionary process driven by natural selection and adaptation. The second feature of the model, the persistent variation in technologies, maintained through entry of new firms and the shock-induced R&D, provides the raw materials which the selection mechanism of market competition operates on. The market selection of firms (and implicitly the technologies) of superior efficiency, as well as the adaptive R&D of individual firms, tends to reduce the degree of technological heterogeneity as firms search their technology space to find the methods of production and operation that would better fit the current technological environment. This process would eventually come to a stop for a given technological environment once all firms have discovered the optimal technology.

The third feature of the model, the persistent shocks which change the optimal technology, keeps the process going by disturbing the collective move toward the technological optimum and re-starting the process of selection and adaptation over and over again. Hence, industry dynamics are characterized by the incessant repetition of external technological shocks, market selection, and the fourth feature, adaptive moves made by firms through R&D investments.

Given the focus on the adaptive behavior of firms and the evolutionary dynamics of industries in the presence of random external shocks, a purely analytical approach based on the standard equilibrium analysis (static or dynamic) would be inappropriate. The computational model developed here forms the basis for an experimental platform on which an artificial industry can be created, evolved, and grown to maturity *in silico*. A wide variety of computational experiments can be performed on this platform, where the time series values of the relevant endogenous variables, both at the individual firm level and at the aggregate industry level, can be generated for close examination.

The analyses of the time series data, reported in this book, shed light on the aforementioned stylized facts in the context of the market interactions among competing firms along the *transient path* of a growing industry. Furthermore, by allowing sufficient time for the industry to grow and mature, the computational platform offers an in-depth look at the adaptive behavior of the firms and the industries along the *stochastic steady state*, i.e., the eventual state in which the endogenous variable capturing the behavior of firms has a time-independent distribution such that the industry fluctuates stochastically around a steady mean. For ease of exposition, such a state will be referred to simply as "steady state." To the extent that the industry-specific factors captured by the relevant parameters in the model determine the developmental trajectory of an industry, the computational platform allows cross-industry comparisons of steady states among industries grown under different parameter specifications. This comparative dynamics exercise provides a test of reliability for the model as the computationally generated outcomes can be compared to the widely accepted results from the cross-sectional studies in the empirical IO literature.

An industry in the model consists of firms having a set of simple decision rules. The rules are driven by the combination of both limited foresight and limited information. Yet, the interactions among these simple rules generate a rich variety of dynamic behavior at the individual level and at the industry level that are consistent with the stylized facts. In particular, the model generates an empirically plausible shakeout pattern for an infant industry. The model also indicates that the behavior of a growing industry on its way to maturity or a fully mature industry in the steady state may be understood as a series of perpetual shakeouts each following an external shock to the firms' technological environment. It turns out that many of the empirical observations involving cross-sectional comparisons among different industries can be explained by way of these repeated shakeouts. The model developed here offers a coherent framework within which these and other stylized facts observed in time series and cross-sectional data on firms and industries can be replicated and understood.

The main causal mechanism for the shakeout phenomenon in the context of the model presented here is the limitation in the ability of firms to foresee the full consequence of their actions. This tends to give rise to excessive entry at the infant stage of the industry. Myopia-induced entries made by a sufficiently large number of firms tend to lead to significant deterioration in the actual realization of the profits for all firms and result in an eventual stampede out of the industry. While the shakeout pattern may seem limited to the infant phase of an industry, the continual shocks to the technological environment can induce a similar pattern to emerge repeatedly as firms are subjected to unanticipated changes in their environment; a *persistent* series of entries and exits arises naturally in the long run.

Given firms with limited foresight, technological diversity, and a technological environment subject to external shocks (features a, b, and c) alone, the eventual fates of firms are determined entirely by the market's selection of those firms having superior production efficiency. However, endogenous R&D by firms, the last feature of the proposed model, gives firms some control over their survival. Endogenous R&D allows firms to *adapt* to the changing environment by seeking technology that may improve their production efficiency. The severity of the recurrent shakeouts is then jointly determined by the size and rate of the external shocks to the technological environment and the intensity with which firms pursue their adaptive R&D.

The plan of the book follows. In Chapter 2, I review the literature on the theoretical approach and the equilibrium-based computational approach to industry dynamics. This review will provide the context in which the choice of the non-equilibrium computational approach used in this book can be justified. An overview of the conceptual framework supporting the proposed model and the detailed description of the model itself are provided in Chapter 3. The model is then put to the test using the baseline configuration of the parameters in Chapter 4. The proto-history for the baseline industry is computationally generated and described in detail.

In Chapter 5, I take on the topic of shakeout in two parts. First, I consider the typical shakeout in an infant industry by abstracting away from the external shocks to the technological environment. The entry and exit decisions are driven purely by the emergence of the profit opportunity in the newly discovered industry; the entry and exit decisions are not influenced by changes in the technological environment. In the second part of the chapter I introduce the external shocks and explore the recurrent shakeouts as they are induced by the changes in the technological environments surrounding firms.

The proposed model allows firms to attain steady states in the long run by allowing sufficient time for the industry to grow and mature. In Chapter 6, I first examine the characteristics of the firm and the industry after the given industry has attained a steady state. I then explore the comparative dynamics by growing industries to maturity under various parameter configurations. Both the intra-industry movements, i.e., changes in the market shares of the firms within the industry, and the inter-industry movements, i.e., entry into and exit out of the industry, of firms are shown to depend on industry-specific factors. The comparative dynamics analysis characterizes the cross-industry differences in volatility in terms of intra- and inter-industry movements.

In Chapter 7, I take a deeper look at the steady state dynamics by observing the endogenous behavior of *individual firms* along the steady state of a given industry. The resulting variations across firms in terms of their technologies, market shares, and life spans are examined.

In the main part of this research I assume market demand to be fixed. In Chapter 8, I allow market demand to fluctuate over time. The endogenous variables at the aggregate level display cyclicality. The emergent patterns are then compared to the stylized facts of cyclical industry dynamics.

Chapter 9 contains the overall summary and conclusions.

Notes

1 See Gort and Klepper (1982), Klepper and Simons (1997, 2000a, 2000b), Carroll and Hannan (2000), Klepper (2002), and Jovanovic and MacDonald (1994).
2 See Dunne et al. (1988).
3 See Dosi and Egidi (1991) for related discussions on "subjective uncertainty" and "procedural uncertainty."

2 Models of industry dynamics

[T]he economist, as opposed to the pure mathematician, must have an ability to understand that from which he abstracts, as well as the abstraction which must be derived from it. Otherwise, when he tries to apply his model, he may concretize his abstractions in ways which bear no relationship to the real world.

[Boulding (1970), p. 114]

IO theorists have used various analytical and numerical approaches to explore the entry and exit dynamics of firms as well as their impacts on the growth of the industry. Many of these models are dynamic in nature and involve heterogeneous firms. However, they also endow the firms, as is standard in current economic theory, with perfect rationality and foresight such that the entry and exit decisions are made to maximize the expected discounted value of future net cash flow.

The pioneering work in this line of research is Jovanovic (1982). He formulated an *equilibrium* model in which new entrants are unsure of their own productivity. Over time, the firms acquire noisy information about their efficiency by engaging in production subject to productivity shocks. The shocks follow a non-stationary process and represent noisy signals that provide evidence to firms about their true costs. The high-cost incumbents receiving sufficiently adverse signals conclude that they are inefficient and withdraw from the market. The "perfect foresight" equilibrium leads to selection through entry and exit in this model. However, once learning is completed, there is no firm turnover in the long run. Consequently, the model is not capable of exploring the patterns in the persistent series of entry and exit as noted in the empirical literature.

Two separate lines of inquiry have developed from the Jovanovic model of industry dynamics. One line continues the purely analytical approach, though the more recent models allow entry and exit to persist in the long run as part of the stationary equilibrium. This approach has been taken by Hopenhayn (1992) and Asplund and Nocke (2006). The second line of inquiry entails incorporating two important features to the original Jovanovic model: 1) "active learning" by the firms; and 2) strategic firm behavior in the framework of oligopolistic rivalry. This line of research employs Markov Perfect Equilibrium as the solution concept; and the equilibrium is solved numerically because of the computational diffi-culty arising from the sheer size of the state space. The relevant papers in this line of research include: Pakes and McGuire (1994), Ericson and Pakes (1995), and Pakes and Ericson (1998), among others.

2.1   Stationary equilibrium models and the purely analytical approach

Hopenhayn (1992) offers an analytically tractable framework, in which perpetual and simultaneous entry and exit are endogenously generated in the long run. This approach entails a dynamic stochastic model of a competitive industry with a continuum of firms. The firms receive indi-vidual productivity shocks each period. Entry and exit of firms are part of the stationary equilibrium he develops in order to analyze the behav-ior of firms along the steady state in the presence of these shocks. The model assumes *perfect competition* and, as such, the stationary equilib-ria maximize net discounted surplus. Hopenhayn finds that changes in aggregate demand do not affect the rate of turnover, though they raise the total number of firms. Asplund and Nocke (2006) point out that the result hinges on the assumption of perfect competition: there is no *price competition effect* induced by the increase in the mass of active firms such that the price-cost margins are independent of market size in this model.

Asplund and Nocke (2006) adopt Hopenhayn's basic framework, but extend it to the case of imperfect competition.[1] To an equilibrium model of entry and exit, they apply the steady state analysis of the type developed by Hopenhayn. Using the reduced-form profit function, they avoid specifying the details of the demand system as well as the nature of the oligopoly competition (e.g., output competition, price competi-tion, price competition with differentiated products, etc.). The key diffe-rence between Hopenhayn's model and their model is that they assume the existence of the *price competition effect* which implies a negative relationship between the number of entrants and the profits of active incumbents. The assumptions made about the reduced-form profit function then lead to two countervailing forces in the model: 1) the rise in market size increases the profits of all firms proportionally through an increase in output levels, holding prices fixed; 2) the total number of firms also increases with the market size, hence reducing the price and the price-cost margin through the *price competition effect*. The main result is that an increase in market size leads to a rise in the turnover rate and a decline in the age distribution of firms in the industry. They provide empirical support for these results using the data on hair salons in Sweden.

It is significant that Asplund and Nocke (2006) were able to generate persistent entry and exit along the steady state of the industry and perform comparative statics analysis with respect to market-specific factors such as market size and the fixed cost. However, their equilibrium approach, while appropriate for the study of the steady state behavior, is inadequate when the focus is on the behavior of firms along the non-equilibrium transitory path – e.g., shakeouts, either during the infancy of the industry or along the adaptive path defining the steady state. In contrast to Asplund and Nocke (2006), the model presented in this book specifies a linear demand function and Cournot output competition. The price competition effect is *generated* as an endogenous outcome of the entry-competition process. Although the functional forms specified in this model are more restrictive than the reduced-form profits approach used by Asplund and Nocke, they are necessary for the task in hand. To examine the effects of the market-specific factors on the evolving structure and performance of the industry, it is imperative that the model fully specify the demand and cost structure so that the relevant variables such as price, outputs, and market shares can be endogenously derived. This allows for a detailed analysis of the firms' behavior along the transitory phase, thus enhancing our understanding of the comparative dynamics properties.

2.2 Markov perfect equilibrium models and the computational approach

Note that learning in Jovanovic's model was "passive" as the firms simply wait for the evidence to come in regarding their true cost. In contrast, Pakes and McGuire (1994), Ericson and Pakes (1995), and Pakes and Ericson (1998) posit "active learning" by producers, where they can affect their own productivity by investing in R&D. The outcomes of R&D are random, however, and those incumbents with a series of adverse shocks find it optimal to exit the market. The solution concept utilized is that of Markov Perfect Equilibrium (MPE) which incorporates strategic decision making by firms with perfect computational

ability and rationality in fully dynamic models of oligopolistic interactions with firm entry and exit – see Pakes and McGuire (1994) and
Ericson and Pakes (1995).

The MPE framework is based on the standard game-theoretic
approach to dynamic oligopoly. As such, it models strategic interactions
among players (firms) who take full account of each other's strategies
and actions. Firms in these models are endowed with perfect rationality: they maximize the expected net present value of future cash flows,
taking into calculation all likely future states of their rivals conditional
on all possible realizations of industry-wide shocks. This implies that
the firms use recursive optimization methodology in their decision making; hence, solving for the equilibrium entails Bellman equations. Given
the degree of complexity in the model specification and the solution
concept involving recursive methods, this approach requires an extensive amount of computation. While this approach is conceptually well
positioned to address the central issues of industry dynamics, its success
has been limited due to the "curse of dimensionality" as described by
Doraszelski and Pakes (2007):

> The computational burden of computing equilibria is large enough
> to often limit the type of applied problems that can be analyzed.
> There are two aspects of the computation that can limit the com-
> plexity of the models we analyze; the computer memory required to
> store the value and policies, and the CPU time required to compute
> the equilibrium .... [I]f we compute transition probabilities as we
> usually do using unordered states then the number of states that we
> need to sum over to compute continuation values grows exponen-
> tially in *both* the number of firms and the number of firm-specific
> state variables.
> [Doraszelski and Pakes (2007), pp. 1915–1916, original emphasis]

The exponential growth of the state space that results from increasing
the number of firms or the set of decision variables imposes a significant
computational constraint on the scale and scope of the research questions one can ask.[2] Furthermore, within a dynamic optimizing model,
analytical results of the MPE approach fall short in various ways in
explaining the empirical regularities.

2.3   Agent-based computational economics approach

The agent-based computational economics (ACE) approach taken in
this book offers a viable alternative to the MPE approach. Tesfatsion
and Judd (2006) provide a succinct description:

ACE is the computational study of economic processes modeled as dynamic systems of interacting agents who do not necessarily possess perfect rationality and information. Whereas standard economic models tend to stress equilibria, ACE models stress economic processes, local interactions among traders and other economic agents, and out-of-equilibrium dynamics that may or may not lead to equilibria in the long run. Whereas standard economic models require a careful consideration of equilibrium properties, ACE models require detailed specifications of structural conditions, institutional arrangements, and behavioral dispositions.

[Tesfatsion and Judd (2006), p. xi]

In a similar vein, my model replaces the standard assumption of perfect foresight and rationality with that of myopia and limited rationality in the firms' decision making. This eliminates the need to evaluate the values and policies for all possible future states for all firms, thus enabling me to avoid the curse of dimensionality inherent in the MPE approach. The computational resources saved are utilized in studying the complex interactions among firms and tracking the movements of relevant endogenous variables over time for a large number of firms. In the present work a reduction in the rationality and foresight of the decision makers enables a more extensive analysis of firm and industry behavior from initial development through maturity in a stochastic environment. The agent-based computational approach thus justifies itself by the increase in the range of issues that can be addressed and the copious and detailed data it can generate in comparison with an MPE model.

The conceptual basis for the ACE model of industry dynamics presented here rests on the evolutionary arguments first advanced by Nelson and Winter (1982) in their seminal work, *An Evolutionary Theory of Economic Change*. In that book, Nelson and Winter developed an evolutionary theory of the behavior of firms and markets as an alternative to the "orthodox" economic theory. The broad theory they develop rejects the notions of perfect rationality and perfect foresight in standard equilibrium models of firms. Instead, Nelson and Winter treat the firms as "motivated by profit and engaged in search for ways to improve their profits, but their actions will not be assumed to be profit maximizing over well-defined and exogenously given choice sets." Their firms are modeled as having "certain capabilities and decision rules" which are modified over time as a result of deliberate learning and random events.

The focus of Nelson and Winter's (1982) work is on the response of firms and industry to changing market conditions *out of equilibrium*.

Assuming firms to have only limited cognitive capacity, they utilize computer simulation as the principal tool for their investigation given the need to trace the exact ways in which the firms' decision rules interact with one another in the market. The ACE model I propose in this book is in full agreement with Nelson and Winter in terms of both the importance given to the process-view of the market competition and the practical choice of simulation methodology as the exploratory tool.

Dawid (2006) provides a comprehensive review of the ACE models that specifically address the issues of innovation and technological change (within the evolutionary framework of Nelson and Winter). He offers two arguments for using the ACE modeling approach in addressing these issues:

> Two main arguments will be put forward to make the point that agent-based models might indeed contribute significantly to this literature. First, as will be argued below, predictions of standard equilibrium models do not provide satisfying explanations for several of the empirically established stylized facts which however emerge quite naturally in agent-based models. Second, the combination of very genuine properties of innovation processes call for a modeling approach that goes beyond the paradigm of a Bayesian representative-agent with full rationality and it seems to me that the possibilities of ACE modeling are well suited to incorporate these properties.
>
> [Dawid (2006), p. 1237]

Both in terms of the methodology and the substance of the issues addressed, the literature surveyed in Dawid (2006) is highly relevant for the work presented in this book. Instead of replicating the survey, I refer the readers to his thorough review.

Much of the agent-based computational work in economics has focused on positive analysis, the main goal being to describe and explain "what is." The same is true of the work reported in this book. However, the real advantage of the agent-based computational approach lies in its potential for normative analysis, given its capacity to perform policy experiments (asking the "what if" questions) with models having substantial institutional details. Efforts in this direction have been made in a number of areas: in public health in the context of designing containment strategies for epidemics (Epstein et al. (2006), Epstein et al. (2011), Parker and Epstein (2011)); in retirement economics (Axtell and Epstein (2006)); in macroeconomic policy design (Dosi et al. (2006, 2008, 2010), Russo et al. (2007), Deissenberg et al. (2008), Mannaro et al. (2008), Neugart (2008), Westerhoff and Dieci (2008)).

In the area of industrial organization, Leigh Tesfatsion and her collaborators have been studying the integrated retail and wholesale (IRW) electric power markets by developing and implementing an agent-based test bed[3] (Sun and Tesfatsion (2007), Li et al. (2011)). The IRW test bed includes the AMES Wholesale Power Market Test Bed as implemented in an open-source software called the *AMES Market Package*. (The acronym, AMES, stands for Agent-based Modeling of Electricity Systems.) The purpose of the AMES test bed is to carry out a systematic experimental study of wholesale power markets as they are restructured in accordance with the US Federal Energy Regulatory Commission's (FERC) market design.

The central feature of their model is the wholesale power market that includes an independent system operator and a group of energy traders (consisting of the load-serving entities and the generation companies distributed across the buses of the transmission grid). The market process is modeled as the multi-period interactions based on demand and supply of the traders, where the generation companies update their action choice probabilities using stochastic reinforcement learning mechanisms. The current version of the model, however, does not allow entry and exit of traders into and out of the wholesale power market. Instead, the traders are allowed to go into debt without being forced to exit.

The AMES model is a showcase for how agent-based computational models can be used for policy experimentation. Although not pursued in this book, the model developed here can pursue similar objectives by asking a wide variety of "what if" questions in the context of antitrust policy and the patent policy as they relate to specific industries. The positive analysis presented in this book is the first step toward addressing those issues.[4]

Notes

1 Melitz (2003) is another extension of Hopenhayn's approach to monopolistic competition, though his focus is on international trade.
2 There have been attempts to circumvent this problem while remaining within the general conceptual framework of the MPE approach. See Weintraub, Benkard, and Van Roy (2008, 2010) for recent works in this line of research.
3 See http://www2.econ.iastate.edu/tesfatsi/IRWProjectHome.htm (accessed September 8, 2014) for a more detailed description of the project as well as a complete list of working papers and publications.

4 See Friedman (1953):

> Normative economics and the art of economics ... cannot be independent of positive economics. Any policy conclusion necessarily rests on a prediction about the consequences of doing one thing rather than another, a prediction that must be based – implicitly or explicitly – on positive economics.
>
> [p. 2]

3 A dynamic model of Schumpeterian competition

> The opening up of new markets, foreign or domestic, and the organizational development from the craft shop to such concerns as US Steel illustrate the same process of industrial mutation – if I may use that biological term – that incessantly revolutionizes the economic structure from within, incessantly destroying the old one, incessantly creating a new one. This process of Creative Destruction is the essential fact about capitalism.
>
> [Schumpeter (1950), p. 83]

The model entails an evolving population of firms which interact with one another through repeated market competition. Central to this process are the heterogeneous production technologies held by the firms and the R&D mechanism through which they evolve over time. I begin the chapter by first discussing the conceptual framework underlying the technological environment within which the firms carry out their R&D activities. The main purpose is to motivate the chosen modeling approach by focusing on a small number of conceptual building blocks; the discussion in this part of the chapter is strictly informal and intuitive, and utilizes simple numerical examples. The preliminary discussion is then followed by a formal presentation of the computational model. The model entails a multi-stage market process in which R&D decisions are made fully endogenous, along with decisions regarding output, entry, and exit.

3.1 Conceptual building blocks

The six building blocks of the model are listed and described as follows:

1. The production process is viewed as a system of activities, where each activity can be accomplished using one of the finite number of methods (practices) specifically available for that activity.

2. A firm's technology is defined by its vector of chosen methods, one method for each component activity of the production process. Assuming two possible methods per activity, a technology is defined by a vector of zeroes and ones.
3. The efficiency of a firm is determined by how closely its technology matches an *ex ante* unknown "optimal technology" uniquely defined for a given technological environment.
4. The degree of a firm's efficiency, as defined above, determines its marginal cost of production.
5. Firms are technologically diverse at any given point in time. The variation in technology choices leads to asymmetry in firms' marginal costs and, consequently, to differential profits attained through market competition.
6. Firms may pursue R&D by experimenting with their technologies – i.e., by altering the method(s) for carrying out one or more of the activities in the production process.

The modeling approach taken in this book offers tangible and quantitative representations of these conceptual building blocks within the dynamic framework of market competition with firm entry and exit.

3.1.1   *Production process as a system of activities*

In this model, a production process is conceptualized as a system of component activities which fit together to confer a certain degree of production efficiency to the firm. In particular, each activity is specified to take on a *finite* number of distinct states, where a given state for an activity represents the practice (method) chosen by the firm for that activity. This approach follows a distinct tradition in the economics and management literature that views activities as the "basic units of competitive advantage" for firms. Milgrom and Roberts (1990), in their study of complementarities in modern manufacturing, emphasize the economic and strategic importance of "activities" in the theory of organizational design.[1] Porter (1996) offers a similar perspective in the context of management strategy.[2]

While issues of complementarities are not the focus of the proposed model, in viewing the process as a system of activities, I am building on the same conceptual foundation. The main modeling issue is how to go from this general perspective to a tangible model which enables us to analyze firm and industry behavior that includes the adaptive use of R&D by firms as they respond to unanticipated shocks to their environment. I start with a stripped down numerical version of the production process and intuitively discuss the concepts of technology, production efficiency, and R&D within its confines.

For concreteness, let us say that the production of a good consists of seven (7) activities. We will call these activities "tasks." Further suppose that each task can be accomplished in a number of different ways, but these ways offer different levels of efficiency. For the sake of expositional simplicity, we will assume that there are two (2) different methods available for each task. In the proposed model, the methods are identified using binary representation. Specifically, given that there are two available methods, we represent them with 0 and 1. Although this example assumes only two ($=2^1$) methods per task, this is without any loss of generality. If we assume that there are four ($=2^2$) possible methods per task, they can be represented with {00, 01, 10, 11}. If there are eight ($=2^3$) possible methods per task, they are represented with {000, 001, 010, 100, 011, 110, 101, 111}. In other words, the total number of methods available per task may be any number that can be expressed as power of 2, and each method can be uniquely identified with a string of bits (0s and 1s).

A typical producer (call it A) of this good, at a given point in time, engages in production by using a vector of methods; one method for each task. For example, it may have chosen to complete the tasks by using the following combination of methods:

Task	#1	#2	#3	#4	#5	#6	#7
Method	0	1	0	0	1	1	0

Hence, it uses method "0" in task #1, method "1" in task #2, method "0" in task #3, and so on. Another producer (B) of the same homogeneous good may choose to complete the same set of tasks using a different combination of methods:

Task	#1	#2	#3	#4	#5	#6	#7
Method	1	1	0	1	0	1	0

These two producers are then using the same methods for tasks #2, #3, #6, and #7, while they use different methods for tasks #1, #4, and #5. Following Porter (1996), any difference in their production efficiencies is then due to those tasks for which these producers are using *different* methods. (In actuality, it should also depend on any interdependence that may exist among a subset of these tasks, but the model proposed here abstracts away from such possibilities by assuming perfect modularity such that there are no interdependencies among these tasks.[3])

The vector of methods then represents the producer's *technology*. Since there are two possible methods for each of the seven tasks, the size of the technology space (from which a technology may be chosen) is $2^7 \cong 128$ – i.e., there is a total of 128 different technologies that could allow a firm to produce the good.

In order to measure the profitability of a firm using a particular technology, we need to assign an efficiency level to each technology in the technology space. The level of efficiency, in turn, determines the firm's marginal cost. Our approach is to assume that there exists a unique vector of methods (common to all firms) that is *optimal* in that it maximizes the overall production efficiency for the firm, given the environment in which the technology is used. As a way of illustration, let us suppose that such a vector involves using method "0" for all tasks:

Task	#1	#2	#3	#4	#5	#6	#7
Optimal method	0	0	0	0	0	0	0

This optimal vector of methods defines the *technological environment* for the firms in that the efficiency of any technology in the technology space is measured in terms of how "close" it is to the optimal vector. To be precise, a firm's production efficiency is assumed to be a decreasing function of the "distance" between its own technology vector and the *optimal* vector, where the distance is defined by the *Hamming distance*, which is the number of positions for which the bits in the two strings (representing the two technologies) differ from one another. With our example the methods used by producer A for tasks #1, #3, #4, and #7 are optimal (same as the *optimal vector*), but those used for tasks #2, #5, and #6 are not, given the technological environment as defined by the above optimal vector. Hence, the Hamming distance is 3 for A as there are three tasks for which its methods deviate from the underlying optimum. For producer B, the distance is then 4. In our context, this implies that producer A is better adapted to the technological environment – i.e., it has superior overall efficiency – than producer B. In the proposed model, the degree of production efficiency (as measured by the Hamming distance) is then transformed into the producer's marginal cost of production through a pre-specified rule (described in 3.2.2).

3.1.2   Change in the technological environment

Given the way the technology space is defined, a change in the technological environment is modeled as a change in the content of the optimal technology vector. This type of change may occur because the technological environment experiences an external shock – e.g., inventions and innovations from other related industries or the introduction of a new regulatory policy, both of which may re-define what are the *best practices* for the given set of activities or tasks within the industry in question. In the proposed model, this is captured by "flipping" one or more bits in the optimal technology vector at the beginning of each period. For instance, the previously defined optimal vector may switch to:

Task	#1	#2	#3	#4	#5	#6	#7
Optimal method	0	0	0	1	0	0	0

Hence, the optimal methods for all tasks remain "0" except for task #4 where method "1" is the new optimum for that task. Such a change reflects a shift in the technological environment and directly affects the efficiencies of the firms. As the result of the change, producer A now experiences a decline in its production efficiency since its Hamming distance to the optimal technology goes up from 3 to 4. On the other hand, producer B sees an improvement in its production efficiency, as its Hamming distance to the optimum goes down from 4 to 3. Whereas A was the more efficient producer in the previous technological environment, the change in the technological environment reverses the relative positions and places B above A.

The proposed model captures this type of technological shift by flipping randomly chosen bits in the optimal technology vector at some pre-specified rate each period. This has the effect of randomly re-shuffling the marginal costs of the competing firms; hence, introducing an element of chance in the evolutionary process of market competition.

3.1.3 Adaptive R&D

The proposed model views the pursuit of R&D as adaptive search, in which the firm explores the technological space to find and adopt a new and improved technology. What is meant by "improvement" in our context is a decline in the Hamming distance between the firm's technology and the prevailing optimal technology. In other words, it is the criterion through which the firm seeks the optimal method for each task in the production process. We assume that the search is a random walk in the technology space (or more accurately a random walk on the efficiency surface mapped from the technology space) to move toward the existing optimum.

Let us go back to the original technological environment in which the optimal method was 0 for all activities. Producer A, given its current technology, may experiment with a different method for task #6 – i.e., changing the method from 1 to 0. The experimental vector under consideration would then be:

Task	#1	#2	#3	#4	#5	#6	#7
Method	0	1	0	0	1	0	0

This potential modification improves the firm's production efficiency, as its Hamming distance to the optimal vector decreases from 3 to 2. Since the idea for the experiment was internally generated (through serendipity or through a costly investment into the R&D effort), this is considered *innovative R&D*.

Alternatively, producer A may have observed producer B, either intentionally or accidentally, and tried to copy B's method in some randomly chosen task, say task #1. Producer B's method in task #1 is "1" and, when copied by producer A, the experimental technology for A becomes:

Task	#1	#2	#3	#4	#5	#6	#7
Method	1	1	0	0	1	1	0

Of course, this makes producer A more similar to producer B; but it also reduces the degree of efficiency for A, since the Hamming distance between this experimental vector under consideration and the optimal technology vector is now 4, which is greater than what it has with its current technology. Hence, the experimental vector should not be adopted. (The evaluation of the technology by a firm is assumed to be done with perfect accuracy. Although it would be preferable to explicitly specify a trial-and-error process as part of the model, the simplifying assumption is made to reduce the computational load.) The act of copying a rival firm's method into one's own set of methods is considered *imitation*. If such a trial results in improving one's efficiency, the imported idea will be implemented and the entire process is referred to as *imitative R&D*.

3.2   The model: basic features

I present in this section the general computational model of industry dynamics with endogenous R&D that fully formalizes the basic ideas described above.

3.2.1 Technology

In each period, firms engage in market competition by producing and selling a homogeneous good. The good is produced through a process that consists of N distinct tasks. Each task can be completed using one of two different methods. Even though all firms produce a homogeneous good, they may do so using different combinations of methods for the N component tasks. The method chosen by the firm for a given task is represented by a bit (0 or 1) such that there are two possible methods available for each task and thus 2^N variants of the production technology. In period t, a firm's *technology* is then fully characterized by a binary vector of N dimensions which captures the complete set of methods it uses to produce the good.

Let $z_i^t \in \{0,1\}^N$ denote firm i's technology in period t, where $z_i^t \equiv (z_i^t(1), z_i^t(2), \ldots, z_i^t(N))$ and $z_i^t(h) \in \{0,1\}$ is firm i's chosen method in task h. In measuring the degree of heterogeneity between two technologies (i.e., method vectors), z_i^t and z_j^t, we use "Hamming distance," which is the number of positions for which the corresponding bits differ:

$$D\left(z_i^t, z_j^t\right) \equiv \sum_{h=1}^{N} \left| z_i^t(h) - z_j^t(h) \right| \tag{3.1}$$

The crucial perspective taken in this model is that the efficiency of a given technology depends on the environment it operates in. In order to represent the technological environment that prevails in period t, I specify a unique methods vector, $\hat{z}^t \in \{0,1\}^N$, which is defined as the *optimal technology* for the industry in t. How well a firm's chosen technology performs in the current environment depends on how close it is to the prevailing optimal technology in the technology space. More specifically, the marginal cost of firm i realized in period t is specified to be a direct function of $D\left(z_i^t, \hat{z}^t\right)$, the Hamming distance between the firm's chosen technology, $\hat{z}_i^t$, and the optimal technology, $\hat{z}^t$. The firms are uninformed about $\hat{z}^t$ *ex ante*, but engage in search to get as close to it as possible by observing their marginal costs. The optimal technology is common for all firms – i.e., all firms in a given industry face the same technological environment. As such, once optimal technology is defined for a given industry, its technological environment is completely specified for all firms since the efficiency of any technology is well-defined as a function of its distance to this optimal technology.

I allow turbulence in the technological environment. Such turbulence is assumed to be caused by factors external to the industry in question such as technological innovations that originate from outside the given industry. In a framework closer to the neoclassical production theory, one could view an externally generated innovation as a shock that affects the relative input prices for the firms. If firms, at any given point in time, are using heterogeneous production processes with varying mix of inputs, such a change in input prices will have diverse impact on the relative efficiencies of firms' production processes – some may benefit from the shock; some may not. Such an external shock will then require (with varying degrees of urgency) a series of adaptive moves by the affected firms for their survival.

The external technology shocks, applied at the beginning of each period, *re-define* firms' production environment and such environmental shifts affect the cost positions of the firms in the competitive marketplace by changing the effectiveness of the methods they use in various activities within the production process. These unexpected disruptions then pose renewed challenges for the firms in their efforts to adapt and survive. It is precisely this kind of external shock that I try to capture in this model. My approach is to allow the optimal technology, $\underline{z}^t$, to vary from one period to the next, where the *frequency* and the *magnitude* of its movement represent the degree of turbulence in the technological environment. The exact mechanism through which this is implemented is described in Section 3.3.1.

Finally, in any given period t, the optimal technology is unique. While the possibility of multiple optimal technologies is a potentially interesting issue, it is not explored here because in a turbulent environment, where the optimal technology is constantly changing, it is likely to be of negligible importance.[4] Chang (2009) offered an alternative approach by modeling the technological environment as being stable but with multiple locally optimal technologies.[5] The main focus was on the industry dynamics during the initial shakeout phase, where one of the objectives was to investigate the impact of multiple optima on the shakeout dynamics. In the current study, I am more interested in the dynamics of R&D and firm turnover in the presence of technological turbulence. As such, I abstract away from the possibility of multiple local optima.   .

3.2.2 Demand, cost, and competition

In each period, there exists a finite number of firms that operate in the market. In this section, I define the static market equilibrium among such firms. The static market equilibrium defined here is then used to *represent* the outcome of market competition in each period.

Let m^t be the number of firms in the market in period t. The firms are Cournot oligopolists, which choose production quantities of a homogeneous good. In defining the Cournot equilibrium in this setting, I assume tentatively that all m^t firms produce positive quantities in equilibrium. This assumption is made strictly for expositional convenience in this section. In actuality, there is no reason to suppose that in the presence of asymmetric costs all m^t firms will produce positive quantities in equilibrium. Some of these firms may choose to be *inactive* by producing zero quantity. The algorithm used to distinguish among active and inactive firms based on their production costs will be addressed in Section 3.3.2.

Demand

The inverse market demand function is:

$$P^t\left(Q^t\right) = a - \frac{Q^t}{s^t} \tag{3.2}$$

where $Q^t = \sum_{j=1}^{m^t} q_j^t$ and s^t denotes the size of the market in t. Note that this function can be inverted to $Q^t = s^t(a - P^t)$. Hence, for a given market price doubling the market size then doubles the quantity demanded. The demand intercept, a, is assumed fixed throughout. (The size parameter, s^t, is also assumed to be fixed throughout the book with the exception of Chapter 8. Chapter 8 examines cyclical industrial dynamics by allowing it to fluctuate.)

Cost

Each firm i at time t has its production technology, z_i^t, and faces the following total cost:

$$C^t\left(q_i^t\right) = f + c_i^t \cdot q_i^t \tag{3.3}$$

All firms have identical fixed cost, f, that stays constant over time.

The firm's marginal cost, c_i^t, depends on how different its technology, z_i^t, is from the optimal technology, $\hat{z}^t$. Specifically, c_i^t is defined as follows:

$$c_i^t(\underline{z}_i^t, \hat{\underline{z}}^t) = 100 \cdot \frac{D(\underline{z}_i^t, \hat{\underline{z}}^t)}{N}. \tag{3.4}$$

Hence, c_i^t increases in the Hamming distance between the firm's chosen technology and the optimal technology for the industry. It is at its minimum of zero when $\underline{z}_i^t = \hat{\underline{z}}^t$ and at its maximum of 100 when all N bits in the two technologies are different from one another. The total cost can be re-written as:

$$C^t\left(q_i^t\right) = f + 100 \cdot \frac{D(\underline{z}_i^t, \hat{\underline{z}}^t)}{N} \cdot q_i^t. \tag{3.5}$$

I assume that the technology does not affect the fixed cost.

Short-run market equilibrium

Given the demand and cost functions, firm i's profit is:

$$\pi_i^t\left(q_i^t, Q^t - q_i^t\right) = \left(a - \frac{1}{s^t}\sum_{j=1}^{m^t} q_j^t\right) \cdot q_i^t - f - c_i^t \cdot q_i^t. \tag{3.6}$$

Taking the first-order condition for each i and summing over m^t firms, we derive the equilibrium industry output rate, which gives us the equilibrium market price, $\bar{P}^t$, through equation (3.2):

$$\bar{P}^t = \left(\frac{1}{m^t+1}\right)\left(a + \sum_{j=1}^{m^t} c_j^t\right). \tag{3.7}$$

Given the vector of marginal costs defined by the firms' chosen technologies and the optimal technology, $\bar{P}^t$ is uniquely determined and is independent of the market size, s^t. Furthermore, the equilibrium market price depends only on the *sum* of the marginal costs and not on the *distribution* of c_i^ts (Bergstrom and Varian (1985)).

The equilibrium firm output rate is:

$$\bar{q}_i^t = s^t\left[\left(\frac{1}{m^t+1}\right)\left(a + \sum_{j=1}^{m^t} c_j^t\right) - c_i^t\right]. \tag{3.8}$$

Note that $\bar{q}_i^t = s^t \left[\bar{P}^t - c_i^t \right]$: A firm's equilibrium output rate depends on its own marginal cost and the market price. Finally, the Cournot equilibrium firm profit is

$$\pi^t \left(\bar{q}_i^t \right) = \bar{P}^t \cdot \bar{q}_i^t - f - c_i^t \cdot \bar{q}_i^t = \frac{1}{s^t} \left(\bar{q}_i^t \right)^2 - f. \tag{3.9}$$

Note that $\bar{q}_i^t$ is a function of c_i^t and $\sum_{j=1}^{m^t} c_j^t$, where c_k^t is a function of z_k^t and $\hat{z}^t$ for all k. It is then straightforward that the equilibrium firm profit is fully determined, once the vectors of methods are known for all firms. Further note that $c_i^t \le c_k^t$ implies $\bar{q}_i^t \ge \bar{q}_k^t$ and, hence, $\pi^t \left(\bar{q}_i^t \right) \ge \pi^t \left(\bar{q}_k^t \right) \forall i, k \in \{1, \dots, m^t\}$.

The use of a Cournot-Nash equilibrium is arguably inconsistent with the "bounded rationality" assumption employed throughout the book. However, explicitly modeling the process of market experimentation would further complicate an already complex model. Therefore, I implicitly assume that experimentation is done instantly and without cost. A Cournot-Nash equilibrium is assumed to be a reasonable approximation of the outcome from that process.[6]

A diversion: static free-entry equilibrium

Before discussing the dynamic structure of the model, it is useful to consider what the purely static version of the above Cournot oligopoly model would imply in terms of the long-run industry equilibrium under free entry and exit as it is typically described in textbooks. For this discussion of the static version, we will dispense with the time superscript for all variables. Also assume that the firms are technologically homogenous so that $c_i^t = c$ for all $i \in \{1, \dots, m\}$. Given m firms, the symmetric Cournot-Nash equilibrium then entails each firm producing the quantity $\bar{q}(m) = \frac{s(a-c)}{m+1}$. The resulting market price is $\bar{P}(m) = \frac{a + mc}{m+1}$. Each firm earns the equilibrium profit, $\bar{\pi}(m) = \frac{s(a-c)^2}{(m+1)^2} - f$.

Note that the equilibrium profit, $\bar{\pi}(m)$, decreases in m. The free-entry equilibrium number of firms, $\bar{m}$, must then satisfy: $\bar{\pi}(\bar{m}+1) < 0 \le \bar{\pi}(\bar{m})$. That is, $\bar{m}$ firms can profitably operate in the industry while $(\bar{m}+1)$ firms cannot. We may define $\bar{m}$ as (the integer part of) m that satisfies $\bar{\pi}(m) = 0$, which is:

$$\bar{m} = (a-c)\sqrt{\frac{s}{f}} - 1. \tag{3.10}$$

Hence, $\bar{m}$ is directly related to the market size (s) and inversely related to the fixed cost (f). In equilibrium, a larger market has a greater number of firms and a market with higher fixed costs has a smaller number of firms.[7]

How does an industry reach the equilibrium structure defined above? The standard description of the out-of-equilibrium adjustment process involves the following story. For all $m < \bar{m}$ the incumbent firms earn positive economic profits and this invites entry into the market thus raising m over time, while for all $m > \bar{m}$ the incumbents incur economic losses and this induces exits from the market thus reducing m over time until the losses are eliminated. In the long run, the industry converges to the stable equilibrium structure containing exactly $\bar{m}$ firms, at which point there is no further entry or exit.

Notice how this implicit mechanism, while guaranteeing the stability of the equilibrium, is incapable of explaining the stylized facts I opened the book with. There are no shakeouts on the way to reaching the stable equilibrium; there are no entries and exits once the industry is in equilibrium; entries and exits, even when they occur out of equilibrium, never occur simultaneously; and there is no plausible story as to why the rates of entry and exit should be higher or lower in a given industry when it is out of equilibrium and what are the causal factors.

It is the lack of explanatory capacity in the standard static model of industry that motivates the dynamic model developed in this book. I introduce persistent external shocks to the technological environment of the firms so as to put the out-of-equilibrium process of entry and exit at the center of the analysis. The pursuit of R&D by firms is made endogenous so that technological heterogeneity (and the consequent cost heterogeneity) becomes an essential part of the industry dynamic. The next section describes how these features are implemented in the model.

3.3   The model: dynamic structure

In the beginning of any typical period t, the industry opens with two groups of decision makers who face a common market environment as specified by the demand size, s^t: 1) a group of incumbent firms surviving from $t-1$, each of whom enters t with a technology, z_i^{t-1}, and its net wealth, w_i^{t-1}, carried over from $t-1$; and 2) a group of potential entrants ready to consider entering the industry in t, each with an endowed technology of $\underline{z}_j^t$ and its start-up wealth. All firms face a common technological environment within which their technology will be used. This environment is fully represented by the prevailing optimal technology, $\hat{\underline{z}}^t$, which is exogenously given to the industry in the beginning of period t. The optimal technology is *ex ante* unknown to the firms and is not necessarily the same as $\hat{\underline{z}}^{t-1}$.

Central to the model is the view that the firms engage in search for the optimal technology over time, but with limited foresight. What makes this "perennial" search non-trivial is the stochastic nature of the production environment – i.e., the technology which was optimal in one period is not necessarily optimal in the next period. This is captured by allowing the optimal technology, $\hat{\underline{z}}^t$, to vary from one period to the next in a systematic manner. The mechanism that guides this shift dynamic is described next.

3.3.1 Turbulence in the technological environment

Consider a binary vector, $\underline{x} \in \{0,1\}^N$. Define $\delta(\underline{x},l) \subset \{0,1\}^N$ as the set of points that are exactly Hamming distance l from $\underline{x}$. The set of points that are *within* Hamming distance l of $\underline{x}$ is then defined as

$$\Delta(\underline{x},l) \equiv U_{i=0}^l \delta(\underline{x},i). \tag{3.11}$$

The following rule governs the shift dynamic of the optimal technology:

$$\hat{\underline{z}}^t = \begin{cases} \hat{\underline{z}}' & \text{with probability } \gamma \\ \hat{\underline{z}}^{t-1} & \text{with probability } 1-\gamma \end{cases}$$

where $\hat{\underline{z}}' \in \Delta(\hat{\underline{z}}^{t-1}, g)$ and γ and g are constant over all t. Hence, with probability γ the optimal technology shifts to a new one within g Hamming distance from the current technology, $\hat{\underline{z}}^{t-1}$, while with probability $1-\gamma$ it remains unchanged at $\hat{\underline{z}}^{t-1}$. The volatility of the technological environment is then captured by γ and g, where γ is the rate and g is the maximum magnitude of changes in technological environment. For the computational experiments reported in this book, $\hat{\underline{z}}'$ is chosen from $\Delta(\hat{\underline{z}}^{t-1}, g)$ according to the uniform distribution.

The change in technological environment is assumed to take place in the beginning of each period before firms make any decisions. While the firms do not know what the optimal technology is for the new

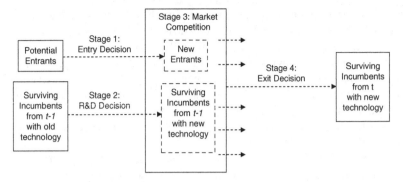

Figure 3.1 Four stages of decision making by firms in period *t*

environment, they are assumed to get accurate signals of their own marginal costs based on the new environment when making their decisions to enter or to perform R&D.[8] This is clearly a strong assumption. A preferred approach would have been to explicitly model the process of learning about the new technological environment; it is for analytical simplicity that I abstract away from this process.

3.3.2   *Multi-stage decision structure*

The technological environment, $\hat{z}^t$, is defined at the start of each period before firms engage in their decision making. Each period consists of four decision stages – see Figure 3.1. Denote by S^{t-1} the set of surviving firms from $t-1$, where $S^0 = \emptyset$. The set of surviving firms includes those firms which were *active* in $t-1$ in that their outputs were strictly positive as well as those firms which were *inactive* with their plants shut down during the previous period. The inactive firms in $t-1$ survive to t if and only if they have sufficient net wealth to cover their fixed costs in $t-1$. Each firm $i \in S^{t-1}$ possesses a production technology, z_i^{t-1}, carried over from $t-1$, which gave rise to its marginal cost of c_i^{t-1} as defined in equation (3.4). It also has the current net wealth of w_i^{t-1} it carries over from $t-1$.

Let R^t denote a finite set of *potential* entrants which contemplate entering the industry in the beginning of t. I assume that the size of the potential entrants pool is fixed and constant at r throughout the entire horizon. I also assume that this pool of r potential entrants is renewed fresh each period. Each potential entrant k in R^t is endowed with a technology, z_k^t, randomly chosen from $\{0,1\}^N$ according to the uniform distribution. In addition, each potential entrant has a fixed start-up wealth with which it enters the market.

Table 3.1 Set notations

Notation	Definition
S^t	Set of surviving firms at the end of t
S^t_+	Those in S^t which were profitable in t
R^t	Set of potential entrants at the beginning of t
E^t	Set of actual entrants in t
M^t	Set of firms poised to compete in t ($= S^{t-1} \cup E^t$)
L^t	Set of firms which exit the industry at the end of t

The definitions of the set notations introduced in this section and used throughout the book are summarized in Table 3.1.

Stage 1: entry decisions

In stage 1 of each period, the potential entrants in R^t first make their decisions to enter. We will denote by b the fixed "start-up" wealth common to all potential entrants. The start-up wealth, b, may be viewed as a firm's available funds that remain after paying for the one-time set-up cost of entry. For example, if one wishes to consider a case where a firm has zero funds available, but must incur a positive entry cost, it would be natural to consider b as having a negative value.

It is important to specify what a potential entrant knows as it makes the entry decision. A potential entrant k knows its own marginal cost, c^t_k, which is based on its technology, z^t_k, and the new environment, $\hat{\underline{z}}^t$: It is not that the potential entrant k knows the content of $\hat{\underline{z}}^t$ (the optimal method for each activity), but only that it gets an accurate signal on c^t_k (which is determined by $\hat{\underline{z}}^t$). The potential entrant also has observations on the market price and the incumbent firms' outputs from $t-1$, i.e., $\bar{P}^{t-1}$ and $\bar{q}^{t-1}_i \forall i \in S^{t-1}$. Given these observations and the fact that $\bar{q}^t_i = s^t[\bar{P}^t - c^t_i]$ from equation (3.8), k can infer c^{t-1}_i for all $i \in S^{t-1}$. While the surviving incumbent's marginal cost in t may be different from that in $t-1$, I assume that the potential entrant takes c^{t-1}_i to stay fixed for lack of information on $\hat{\underline{z}}^t$. The potential entrant k then uses c^t_k and $\left\{ c^{t-1}_i \right\}_{\forall i \in S^{t-1}}$ in computing the post-entry profit expected in t. Table 3.2 summarizes the decision environment for the potential entrants as well as for the incumbents.

Given the above information, the entry rule for a potential entrant takes the simple form that it will be attracted to enter the industry if and only if it perceives its post-entry net wealth in period t to be strictly

Table 3.2 Beliefs underlying the firms' decision-making

Potential entrant (k)	All $k \in R^t$
Given	Market size: s^t
	Technological environment: $\hat{z}^t$
	Endowed technology: $\underline{z}_k^t$
Beliefs	Set of players: $S^{t-1} \cup k$
	Marginal costs: $c_i^{t-1} \forall i \in S^{t-1}$ and c_k^t for k
Compute	Expected profit: $\pi_k^e(\underline{z}_k^t)$
Surviving incumbents (j)	*All $j \in S^{t-1}$*
Given	Market size: s^t
	Technological environment: $\hat{z}^t$
	Current technology: z_j^{t-1}
Beliefs	Set of players: S^{t-1}
	Marginal costs: $c_i^{t-1} \forall i \in S^{t-1}$
Compare	c_j^{t-1} and $\tilde{c}_j^t$

positive. The entry decision then depends on the profit that it expects to earn in t following entry, which is assumed to be the static Cournot equilibrium profit based on the marginal costs of the active firms from $t-1$ and itself as the only new entrant in the market. That each potential entrant assumes itself to be the only firm to enter is clearly a strong assumption. Nevertheless, this assumption is made for two reasons. First, it has the virtue of simplicity. Second, Camerer and Lovallo (1999) provide support for this assumption by showing in an experimental setting of business entry that most subjects who enter tend to do so with overconfidence and excessive optimism. Furthermore, they find:

> Excess entry is much larger when subjects volunteered to participate knowing that payoffs would depend on skill. These self-selected subjects seem to neglect the fact that they are competing with a reference group of subjects who all think they are skilled too.
>
> [Camerer and Lovallo (1999), p. 307]

The decision rule of a potential entrant $k \in R^t$ is then:

$$\begin{cases} Enter, & if\ and\ only\ if\ \ \pi_k^e\left(\underline{z}_k^t\right) + b > \underline{W}; \\ Stay\ out, & otherwise \end{cases} \quad (3.12)$$

where π_k^e is the static Cournot equilibrium profit the entrant *expects* to make in the period of its entry and $\underline{W}$ is the threshold level of wealth for a firm's survival (common to all firms).

Once every potential entrant in R^t makes its entry decision on the basis of the above criterion, the resulting set of *actual* entrants, $E^t \subseteq R^t$, contains only those firms with sufficiently efficient technologies to guarantee some threshold level of profits given every potential entrant's belief about the market structure and the technological environment. Denote by M^t the set of firms ready to compete in the industry: $M^t \equiv S^{t-1} \cup E^t$.

At the end of stage 1 of period t, we have a well-defined set of competing firms, M^t, with their current net wealth, $\{w_i^{t-1}\}_{\forall i \in M^t}$ and their technologies, z_i^{t-1} for all $i \in S^{t-1}$ and z_j^t for all $j \in E^t$.

Stage 2: R&D decisions

In stage 2, the surviving incumbents from $t-1, S^{t-1}$, engage in R&D to improve the efficiency of their existing technologies. Given that the entrants in E^t entered with new technologies, they do not engage in R&D in t. In addition, only those firms with sufficient wealth to cover the R&D expenditure engage in R&D. I will denote by I_i^t the R&D expenditure incurred by firm i in t.

The R&D process transforms the incumbent's technology from z_i^{t-1} to z_i^t, where $z_i^t = z_i^{t-1}$ if either no R&D is performed in t or R&D is performed but its outcome is not adopted. The modeling of this transformation process is described separately and in full detail in Section 3.3.3.

Stage 3: output decisions and market competition

Given the R&D decisions made in stage 2 by the firms in S^{t-1}, all firms in M^t now have the updated technologies $\{z_i^t\}_{\forall i \in M^t}$. With the updated technologies, the firms engage in Cournot competition in the market, where we represent the outcome with the Cournot equilibrium defined in Section 3.2.2.

Recall that the equilibrium in Section 3.2.2 was defined for m^t firms under the assumption that all m^t firms produce positive quantities. In actuality, given the asymmetric costs, there is no reason to think that all firms in M^t will produce positive quantities in equilibrium. Some relatively inefficient firms may shut down their plants and stay inactive (but still pay the fixed cost). What we need is a mechanism for identifying the set of *active* firms out of M^t such that the Cournot equilibrium among these firms will indeed entail positive quantities only. This is done in the following sequence of steps. Starting from the initial set of active firms, compute the equilibrium outputs for each firm. If the outputs for one or more firms are negative, then de-activate the least efficient firm from the set of currently active firms, i.e., set $q_i^t = 0$ where i is the least efficient firm. Re-define the set of active firms (as the previous set of active firms minus the de-activated firms) and recompute the equilibrium outputs. Repeat the procedure until all active firms are producing non-negative outputs. Each *inactive* firm produces zero output and incurs the economic loss equivalent to its fixed cost. Each *active* firm produces its equilibrium output and earns the corresponding profit. We then have π_i^t for all $i \in M^t$.

Stage 4: exit decisions

Given the single-period profits or losses made in stage 3 of the game, the firms in M^t consider exiting the industry in the final stage. Each firm's net wealth is first updated on the basis of the profits (or losses) made in stage 3 as well as the R&D expenditure incurred in stage 2:[9]

$$w_i^t = w_i^{t-1} + \pi_i^t - I_i^t \tag{3.13}$$

where I_i^t is the firm's R&D expenditure made in stage 2. The exit decision rule for each firm is then:

$$\begin{cases} Stay\,in, & if\,and\,only\,if\,w_i^t \geq \underline{W}; \\ Exit, & otherwise; \end{cases} \tag{3.14}$$

where $\underline{W}$ is the previously defined threshold level of net wealth such that all firms with their current net wealth below $\underline{W}$ exit the market. Define L^t as the set of firms which exit the market in t. Once the exit decisions are made by all firms in M^t, the set of surviving firms from period t is then defined as:

$$S^t \equiv \{all\,i \in M^t | w_i^t \geq \underline{W}\}. \tag{3.15}$$

The set of surviving firms, S^t, their current technologies, $\{z_i^t\}_{\forall i \in S^t}$, and their current net wealth, $\{w_i^t\}_{\forall i \in S^t}$, are then passed on to $t+1$ as state variables.

Prior work using the base model

Variants of the model, as described above, have been used in two previously published papers, Chang (2009, 2011). In both papers, the second stage R&D activity was assumed to be *exogenous* and *costless*. More specifically, R&D was viewed as a serendipitous discovery, in which the methods used in one or more of the tasks were randomly altered each period for experimentation. Chang (2009) assumed a stable technological environment in which the optimal technology did not change from one period to next, i.e., $\gamma = 0$. Instead, the technology itself was assumed to be *complex* in nature such that there were multiple optima. The main focus was on the *shakeout* phase of an industry's life cycle, immediately following its birth. The model generated shakeout patterns consistent with empirical observations.

Chang (2011) allowed turbulence in the technological environment as in this book, i.e., $\gamma > 0$. The focus was on the long-run steady state in which continual series of entries and exits were observed. Consistent with the available empirical findings (Dunne et al., 1988), the model generated persistent series of entries and exits. Also consistent with empirical observations, the contemporary rates of entry and exit were shown to be positively correlated. Comparing the turnover rates across industries with different market-specific characteristics, it was found that the mean rates of entry and exit move together across all industries. An industry with a higher-than-average rate of entry is also likely to have a higher-than-average rate of exit. Further delving into how market-specific factors affect the turnover rates of the firms and, consequently, the steady-state market structure, Chang (2011) found that the *rate* of firm turnover and the industry concentration are positively related.[10] All of these results continue to hold with the present model where R&D is endogenous.

Both papers provided the foundation on which to build the model of industry dynamics. Validation of the model was achieved by generating results that were consistent with the empirical observations. Nevertheless, these earlier models were inadequate as the model of Schumpeterian competition because the R&D process was specified to be exogenous. The model presented here makes the R&D decisions fully endogenous so as to study the relationship between R&D and firm turnovers in a unified model of *creative destruction* as envisioned by Schumpeter.

3.3.3 *Making the process of R&D endogenous*

If we knew what it was we were doing, it would not be called research, would it?

[Albert Einstein]

The process of R&D is made endogenous in this model. This process corresponds to the stage-2 process of transforming z_i^{t-1} to z_i^t as described

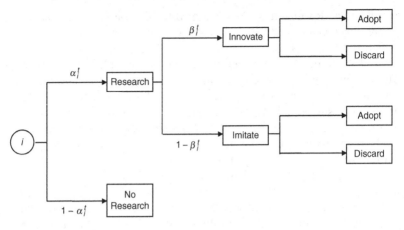

Figure 3.2 Sequence of R&D decisions within stage 2

in Section 3.3.2. I model the R&D-related decisions as being driven by a set of choice probabilities that evolve over time on the basis of a reinforcement learning mechanism. If a firm decides to pursue R&D, it can do so through either *innovation* or *imitation*. The size of R&D expenditure depends on which of the two modes a given firm chooses: *Innovation* costs a fixed amount of K_{IN} while *imitation* costs K_{IM}. Hence, the sufficient condition for a firm to engage in R&D is to have enough net wealth to cover the maximum R&D expense:

$$w_i^{t-1} \geq \max\{K_{IN}, K_{IM}\}. \tag{3.16}$$

In the computational experiments reported in this book I assume $K_{IN} > K_{IM}$.

Figure 3.2 illustrates the various stages of the R&D process. The crucial part of this model is how the various components of the R&D decision are carried out. First, each firm i has two probabilities, α_i^t and β_i^t, which evolve over time via a reinforcement learning mechanism. Each period, firm i chooses to pursue R&D with probability α_i^t and not to pursue R&D with probability $1 - \alpha_i^t$. If the firm chooses not to pursue R&D, it simply keeps the old technology and, hence, $z_i^t = z_i^{t-1}$. However, if the firm chooses to pursue R&D, then it has a probability β_i^t with which it chooses to "innovate" and $1 - \beta_i^t$ with which it chooses to "imitate." (As mentioned, both α_i^t and β_i^t are endogenous – how they are updated from one period to the next is discussed below.)

Innovation occurs when the firm considers changing the method (i.e., flipping the bit) in *one* randomly chosen activity. *Imitation* occurs when the firm (i) picks another firm (j) from a subset of S^{t-1} and considers copying the method employed by j in *one* randomly chosen activity while retaining his (i's) current methods in all other activities. (Hence, the imitating firm is capable of copying only a small part of the entire technology.[11])

Only those surviving firms which were profitable in $t-1$, i.e., $\pi_k^{t-1} > 0$, are considered as potential targets for imitation. Let S_+^{t-1} denote the set of these *profitable* firms, where $S_+^{t-1} \subseteq S^{t-1}$. The choice of a firm to imitate is made probabilistically using the "roulette wheel" algorithm. To be specific, the probability of firm $i \in S^{t-1}$ observing a firm $j \in S_+^{t-1}$ is denoted p_{ij}^t and is defined as follows:

$$p_{ij}^t = \pi_j^{t-1} / \left(\sum_{\forall k \in S_+^{t-1}, k \neq i} \pi_k^{t-1} \right) \qquad (3.17)$$

such that $\sum_{\forall j \in S_+^{t-1}, j \neq i} p_{ij}^t = 1 \forall i \in S^{t-1}$. Hence, the more profitable firm is more likely to be imitated.

Let $\tilde{z}_i^t$ denote firm i's vector of experimental methods (i.e., a technology considered for potential adoption) obtained through *innovation* or through *imitation*. The adoption decision rule is as follows:

$$z_i^t = \begin{cases} \tilde{z}_i^t, & \text{if and only if } c_i\left(\tilde{z}_i^t, \hat{z}^t\right) < c_i\left(z_i^{t-1}, \hat{z}^t\right); \\ z_i^{t-1}, & \text{otherwise.} \end{cases} \qquad (3.18)$$

Firm i adopts the proposed technology if and only if it lowers the marginal cost below the level attained with the current technology the firm carries over from the previous period.[12] Hence, adoption happens when the Hamming distance to the optimal technology is lower with the proposed technology than with the current technology. Notice that this condition is equivalent to a condition on the firm profitability. When an incumbent firm takes all other incumbent firms' marginal costs as given, the only way that its profit is going to improve is if its marginal cost is reduced as the result of its R&D.

Note that firm i's R&D expenditure in period t depends on the type of R&D activity it pursues:

$$
I_i^t = \begin{cases} 0 & \text{if no R \& D was pursued;} \\ K_{IN} & \text{if R \& D was pursued and innovation was chosen;} \\ K_{IM} & \text{if R \& D was pursued and imitation was chosen.} \end{cases} \quad (3.19)
$$

Let us get back to the choice probabilities, α_i^t and β_i^t. Both probabilities are endogenous and specific to each firm. Specifically, they are adjusted over time by individual firms according to a reinforcement learning rule. I adopt a version of the *Experience-Weighted Attraction (EWA)* learning rule as described in Camerer and Ho (1999). Under this rule, a firm has a numerical *attraction* for each possible course of action. The learning rule specifies how attractions are updated by the firm's experience and how the probabilities of choosing different courses of action depend on these attractions. The main feature is that a positive outcome realized from a course of action reinforces the likelihood of that same action being chosen again.

Formally, the choice probabilities, α_i^t and β_i^t, are determined by the attraction measures, $(A_i^t, \bar{A}_i^t)$ and $(B_i^t, \bar{B}_i^t)$, as follows:

$$
\alpha_i^t = \frac{A_i^t}{A_i^t + \bar{A}_i^t}; \beta_i^t = \frac{B_i^t}{B_i^t + \bar{B}_i^t}, \quad (3.20)
$$

where A_i^t is the attraction for *R&D* and $\bar{A}_i^t$ is the attraction for *No R&D*, while B_i^t is the attraction for *Innovation* and $\bar{B}_i^t$ is the attraction for *Imitation*.

At the end of each period, α_i^t and β_i^t are adjusted on the basis of the changing values for these attraction measures. Table 3.3 shows the adjustment dynamics of these attractions for the entire set of possible cases. According to this rule, A_i^t is raised by a unit when R&D (either through innovation or imitation) was productive and the generated idea was adopted. Alternatively, $\bar{A}_i^t$ is raised by a unit when R&D was unproductive and the generated idea was discarded.

In terms of the choice between innovation and imitation, B_i^t is raised by a unit if R&D via innovation was performed and the generated idea was adopted or if R&D via imitation was performed and the generated idea was discarded. Hence, the attraction for innovation can increase if either innovation was productive or imitation was unproductive. Conversely, $\bar{B}_i^t$ is raised by a unit if R&D via imitation generated an idea which was adopted – i.e., imitation was productive – or R&D via innovation generated an idea which was discarded – i.e., innovation

Table 3.3 Evolving attractions

Decision path			Updating of attractions			
No R&D			$A_i^{t+1} = A_i^t;$	$\bar{A}_i^{t+1} = \bar{A}_i^t;$	$B_i^{t+1} = B_i^t;$	$\bar{B}_i^{t+1} = \bar{B}_i^t;$
R&D	Innovate	Adopt	$A_i^{t+1} = A_i^t + 1;$	$\bar{A}_i^{t+1} = \bar{A}_i^t;$	$B_i^{t+1} = B_i^t + 1;$	$\bar{B}_i^{t+1} = \bar{B}_i^t;$
		Discard	$A_i^{t+1} = A_i^t;$	$\bar{A}_i^{t+1} = \bar{A}_i^t + 1;$	$B_i^{t+1} = B_i^t;$	$\bar{B}_i^{t+1} = \bar{B}_i^t + 1;$
	Imitate	Adopt	$A_i^{t+1} = A_i^t + 1;$	$\bar{A}_i^{t+1} = \bar{A}_i^t;$	$B_i^{t+1} = B_i^t;$	$\bar{B}_i^{t+1} = \bar{B}_i^t + 1;$
		Discard	$A_i^{t+1} = A_i^t;$	$\bar{A}_i^{t+1} = \bar{A}_i^t + 1;$	$B_i^{t+1} = B_i^t + 1;$	$\bar{B}_i^{t+1} = \bar{B}_i^t;$

was unproductive. If no R&D was performed, all attractions remain unchanged.

Finally, all new entrants in E^t are endowed with the initial attractions that make them indifferent to the available options at the time of their entry. Specifically, I assume that $A_i^t = \bar{A}_i^t = 10$ and $B_i^t = \bar{B}_i^t = 10$ for new entrants such that $\alpha_i^t = \beta_i^t = 0.5$ for all i – i.e., all new entrants have equal probabilities of choosing between *R&D* and *No R&D* as well as between *innovation* and *imitation*. Of course, these attractions will eventually diverge from one another as the firms go through different market experiences as the result of their R&D decisions made over time.

Notes

1 See Milgrom and Roberts (1990):

> Here, we use the term "complements" not only in its traditional sense of a relation between *pairs of inputs*, but also in a broader sense as a relation among *groups of activities*. The defining characteristic of these groups of complements is that if the levels of any subset of the activities are increased, then the marginal return to increases in any or all of the remaining activities rises. It then follows that if the marginal costs associated with some activities fall, it will be optimal to increase the level of all of the activities in the grouping.
>
> [p. 514, original emphasis]

2 See Porter (1996):

> Ultimately, all differences between companies in cost or price derive from the hundreds of activities required to create, produce, sell, and deliver their products or services, such as calling on customers, assembling final products, and training employees. Cost is generated by performing activities, and cost advantage arises from performing particular activities more efficiently than competitors. Similarly, differentiation arises from both the choice of activities and how they are performed. Activities, then, are the basic units of competitive advantage. Overall advantage or disadvantage results from all a company's activities, not only a few.
>
> [p. 62]

3 This system-of-activities approach takes its origin from the NK-model of Kauffman (1993). The original NK-model was meant for addressing the issue of "complexity" that arises from the interdependence among a subset of activities. While the proposed model is fully capable of incorporating such feature, my focus is more on the properties of industry dynamics and market competition. As such, I assume a "simple" production process by specifying the component activities to be distinct from one another with no mutual interdependence. An implication of this assumption is that there is a "unique" optimum in the technology space. Chang (2009), however, undertook the investigation of production complexity and how it affects the shakeout dynamics of an infant industry. The model in that work uses the original NK-model as introduced by Kauffman. The presence of interdependence among activities leads to multiple optima in the technology space.

4 The issue of multiple optima was, in fact, the focus of the literature on complementarities in manufacturing. See Milgrom and Roberts (1990) and Porter (1996).

5 Multiple optima arise naturally when the production process is assumed to be complex – i.e., some or all of the activities are mutually interdependent (Kauffman (1993)).

6 There are results from the experimental economics literature that do support this rather heroic assumption. In their pioneering work, Fouraker and Siegel (1963) conducted experiments with participants who took the role of quantity-adjusting Cournot oligopolists under incomplete information. They found that the Cournot-Nash equilibrium was supported in many trials for the cases of duopoly and triopoly. Similarly, Cox and Walker (1998), using linear demand and constant marginal cost in Cournot duopoly, found that, if a stable equilibrium exists, then the participants in their experiments learn to play the Cournot-Nash equilibrium after only a few periods. Even though the best reply dynamics do not necessarily converge in oligopolies with more than three firms (Theocharis (1960)), Huck et al. (1999) finds that the best reply process does converge if firms are assumed to exhibit some *inertia* in their choice of strategy. For a more general discussion and survey of the literature involving experimental treatment of oligopoly behavior, please see Armstrong and Huck (2010).

7 It is shown in Chapter 6 that the dynamic model presented in this book does predict the same relationships along the steady state when the industry is subject to persistent technology shocks.

8 It should be noted that more than one optimal technology can yield the same marginal cost for the firm given its technology.

9 It does not matter whether R&D expenditure is subtracted from the net wealth in stage 2 or in stage 4. It is a sunk cost by the time market competition starts and, as such, it has no impact on the firm's output decision in stage 3.

10 The rate of turnover is the number of entries (or exits) relative to the total number of operating firms.

11 This is one aspect of the cognitive limitation assumed in this research. An issue that can be investigated in the future is to relax this assumption and examine the impact that a firm's cognitive capacity has on the various outcomes at the firm and industry level. This is not pursued here.

12 I assume that the evaluation of the technology by a firm in terms of its production efficiency (as represented by the level of its marginal cost) is done with perfect accuracy. While this assumption is clearly unrealistic, it is made to avoid overloading the model.

4 Growing an industry *in silico*

Everything is the way it is because it got that way.
[Frequently attributed to D'Arcy Wentworth Thompson]*

The computational approach taken in this study allows us to perform controlled experiments by "creating and growing" an industry *in silico*.[1] The procedure starts with an empty industry – i.e., $S^0 = \emptyset$. The "birth" of the industry is signified by the initial group of firms which enter the industry in $t = 1$. The market competition following their entry determines the set of surviving incumbents which, along with a fresh set of potential entrants, undergo the multi-stage decision process described in Chapter 3. The dynamic interaction between the turbulent technological environment and the multi-agent decision process drives the growth and development of the industry in the long run.

In this chapter, I specify the parameter values for a baseline case, and describe the various parameter configurations considered in the study as a whole. I also describe the endogenous variables that are tracked for analyses and provide a visual display of the growth and development path taken by an industry characterized by the baseline parameter configuration. The baseline provides a useful benchmark for the comparative dynamics analyses performed in the following chapters.

4.1 Design of computational experiments

A particular industry is characterized by the set of parameters specified in the model. The values of the parameters used in this study, including those for the baseline simulation, are provided in Table 4.1.

The production process is specified to have 96 separate tasks ($N = 96$), where the method chosen for each task is represented by a single bit. This implies that there are $2^{96} \left(\cong 8 \times 10^{28} \right)$ different combinations of methods

Table 4.1 List of parameters and their values

Notation	Definition	Baseline value	All values
N	Number of tasks	96	96
r	Number of potential entrants per period	40	40
b	Start-up wealth for a new entrant	0	0
$\underline{W}$	Threshold net wealth for survival	0	0
a	Demand intercept	300	300
f	Fixed production cost	200	{200, 300, 400, 500}
K_{IN}	Fixed cost of innovation	100	{100, 300, 500, 700}
K_{IM}	Fixed cost of imitation	50	{50, 150, 250, 350}
A_i^0	Initial attraction for R&D	10	10
$\bar{A}_i^0$	Initial attraction for no R&D	10	10
B_i^0	Initial attraction for innovation	10	10
$\bar{B}_i^0$	Initial attraction for imitation	10	10
T	Time horizon	5,000	5,000
s	Market size when demand does not fluctuate	4	{3, 4, 5, 6}
γ	Rate of change in technological environment	0.1	{0, 0.1}
g	Maximum magnitude of change in technological environment	8	8

for the complete production process. In each period, there are exactly 40 potential entrants that consider entering the industry, where a new firm enters with a start-up wealth (b) of zero. An incumbent firm will exit the industry if its net wealth falls below the threshold level ($\underline{W}$) of zero. The demand intercept (a) is fixed at 300. With the exception of the analysis carried out in Chapter 7, the cost of innovation, K_{IN}, is fixed at 100, while the cost of imitation, K_{IM}, is fixed at 50. In Chapter 7, we examine the impact of the costs of R&D by considering four distinct pairs of K_{IN} and K_{IM}: $(K_{IN}, K_{IM}) \in \{(100,50),(300,150),(500,250),(700,350)\}$.

All initial attractions for R&D activities are such that the new entrants are indifferent between *R&D* and *No R&D* ($A_i^0 = \bar{A}_i^0 = 10$) as well as between *Innovation* and *Imitation* ($B_i^0 = \bar{B}_i^0 = 10$). The rate of change in the technological environment is set at $\gamma = 0.1$. The maximum magnitude of a change in technological environment, g, is held fixed at 8 – i.e., the Hamming distance between the optimal technologies at $t - 1$

and at t cannot be more than 8 bits. The time horizon (T) is over 5,000 periods, where in period 1 the market starts out empty. The examination of the simulation outputs shows that the horizon of 5,000 periods is more than enough for an industry to achieve a steady state for all parameter values considered in this research.

For the analyses of the baseline and the long-run steady state, I fix the size of the market over time such that $s^t = s$ for all t. The market size will be allowed to fluctuate in Chapter 8 in order to study the cyclical dynamics of the industry in the presence of fluctuating demand. In this and the next three chapters, the focus of my analysis is on the impacts of the market size (s) and the fixed cost (f) on the industry dynamics. I consider four different values for the two parameters: $s \in \{3,4,5,6\}$ and $f \in \{200,300,400,500\}$.

Starting from an empty industry with the above configuration of parameters, I evolve the industry and trace its development by keeping track of the following endogenous variables:

- $|E^t|$: number of firms that entered the industry in the beginning of t;
- $|L^t|$: number of firms that left the industry at the end of t;
- $|M^t|$: number of firms that were in the industry in t (including both active and inactive firms);
- $|S^t|$: number of firms that survived at the end of $t (=|M^t| - |L^t|)$;
- P^t: market price at which goods were traded in t;
- $\{c_i^t\}_{\forall i \in M^t}$: realized marginal costs of all firms in the industry in t;
- $\{q_i^t\}_{\forall i \in M^t}$: actual outputs of all firms in the industry in t;
- $\{\pi_i^t\}_{\forall i \in M^t}$: realized profits (or losses) of all firms in the industry in t;
- $\{age_i^t\}_{\forall i \in M^t}$: ages of all firms in the industry in t;
- $\{\alpha_i^t\}_{\forall i \in M^t}$: *R&D* intensities of all firms in the industry in t;
- $\{\beta_i^t\}_{\forall i \in M^t}$: *innovation* intensities of all firms in the industry in t;
- $\{I_i^t\}_{\forall i \in M^t}$: R&D spending of all firms in the industry in t ($I_i^t = 0$ if a firm did not perform any R&D; $I_i^t = K_{IN}$ if firm i performed innovation; $I_i^t = K_{IM}$ if firm i performed imitation).

Using the above variables, I construct an additional group of endogenous variables that characterize the aggregate behavior of the firms in an industry. First, denote by Q^t and Π^t the aggregate output and the aggregate profit of all firms in period t: $Q^t = \sum_{\forall j \in M^t} q_j^t$ and $\Pi^t = \sum_{\forall j \in M^t} \pi_j^t$.

Note that both the size of the market (s) and the fixed cost (f) are likely to have significant influence on the number of firms that a given industry can sustain in the long run. Since the magnitude of firm turnovers must be viewed in relation to the size of the industry, I construct the *rates* of entry and exit, ER^t and XR^t, which are, respectively, the number of new entrants and the number of exiting firms as the fractions of the total number of firms in period t:

$$ER^t = \frac{|E^t|}{|M^t|} \text{ and } XR^t = \frac{|L^t|}{|M^t|}. \tag{4.1}$$

The rate of firm survival in period t is then $1 - XR^t$.

As a concentration measure, I use the Herfindahl-Hirschmann Index, H^t:

$$H^t = \sum_{\forall i \in M^t} \left(\frac{q_i^t}{Q^t} * 100 \right)^2. \tag{4.2}$$

A novel aspect of the model is how technological heterogeneity leads to cost asymmetries among firms. To investigate the evolving technological heterogeneity within the industry, I introduce a measure of the "degree of technological diversity," DIV^t. It is defined as the ratio of the mean technological difference in the population of all firms to the maximum possible difference. To be specific, first note that the maximum difference between any two technologies is when their Hamming distance is N. The mean Hamming distance, the numerator of the ratio, is computed as an average of the *Hamming* distances between all distinct pairs of firms within the population. Since the set of firms, M^t, contains a total of $|M^t|$ firms, the total number of distinct pairs that can be formed among them is: $\frac{1}{2}|M^t|(|M^t|-1)$. The degree of technological diversity is then computed as:

$$DIV^t = \frac{2}{N|M^t|(|M^t|-1)} \sum_{\substack{\forall i,j \in M^t \\ i \neq j}} D\left(z_i^t, z_j^t\right). \tag{4.3}$$

The practical implication of the heterogeneity in firms' technologies is the asymmetry it creates in terms of their production efficiency and the consequent market shares. Note that in each period t, the market share of a firm i is defined as $\frac{q_i^t}{Q^t}$. The inequality in market shares in t may then be represented by the *Gini* coefficient, G^t, which is computed as:

$$G^t = \frac{2\sum_{i=1}^{|M^t|}\left(i * \frac{q_i^t}{Q^t}\right)}{|M^t|} - \frac{|M^t|+1}{|M^t|}.$$

(4.4)

To examine the aggregate intensity of the R&D activities, I look at the total R&D spending in the industry, TRD^t:

$$TRD^t = \sum_{\forall i \in M^t} I_i^t.$$

(4.5)

If a firm pursues R&D, it either innovates or imitates. The aggregate R&D expenditure, $\sum_{\forall i \in M^t} I_i^t$, in period t then consists of the amount spent by the firms that innovate and the amount spent by those that imitate. (It should be noted that the inactive firms, producing zero output while paying the fixed cost, may still choose to pursue R&D and incur these expenses if they have sufficient net wealth.) Denote by TCN^t the aggregate amount spent on *innovation* (rather than imitation) by all firms in period t. Let NRD^t be the cost share of innovation in the aggregate R&D spending:

$$NRD^t = \frac{TCN^t}{TRD^t}.$$

(4.6)

NRD^t, hence, measures the industry's relative tendency to invest in innovation rather than in imitation.

For an aggregate measure of the industry's production efficiency, I construct an industry marginal cost, WMC^t, where

$$WMC^t = \sum_{\forall i \in M^t}\left[\left(\frac{q_i^t}{Q^t}\right) * c_i^t\right].$$

(4.7)

WMC^t is, hence, the weighted average of the individual firms' marginal costs in period t, where the weights are the market shares of the firms in that period.

In order to evaluate the market power of the firms, I also construct an aggregate measure of firms' price-cost margins, PCM^t, where

$$PCM^t = \sum_{\forall i \in M^t}\left[\left(\frac{q_i^t}{Q^t}\right) * \left(\frac{P^t - c_i^t}{P^t}\right)\right].$$

(4.8)

PCM^t is the weighted average of the individual firms' price-cost margins in period t, where the weights are the market shares of the firms.

For a measure of consumer welfare, I compute the consumer surplus as the usual triangular area under the demand curve above the market price:

$$CS^t = \frac{1}{2}(a - P^t)Q^t, \tag{4.9}$$

where P^t and Q^t are the realized price and aggregate output in period t.

Finally, the total surplus that captures the overall social welfare is computed as the sum of consumer surplus and the aggregate profit:

$$TS^t = CS^t + \Pi^t. \tag{4.10}$$

4.2 The baseline: generating the proto-history

The first step in my analysis is to examine the evolving structure of a typical industry as characterized by the baseline parameter values indicated in Table 4.1. The baseline case discussed here, as well as the cases examined for comparative dynamics analyses in Chapters 5–7, assumes that the market demand is completely fixed and, hence, $s^t = \hat{s}(= 4)$ for all t. Any shift in the firms' decision environment is solely due to the random shocks in the technological environment. The external technological shocks induce entry and exit of firms by directly influencing their current marginal costs, but they also give rise to adaptive R&D by firms in their search for the new technological optimum. After the initial transition period following its birth, the industry settles into a steady state in which each endogenous variable representing the industry structure fluctuates around a constant mean with a finite variance.

I start by focusing on a single randomly chosen replication and observing the endogenous time paths of the three turnover variables over the 5,000 periods of the industry's development from its birth to full maturity: (a) the number of entrants, $|E^t|$; (b) the number of exiting firms, $|L^t|$; and (c) the total number of firms, $|M^t|$. The results are captured in Figure 4.1.

Note from Figure 4.1(a) the initial surge in the number of new entrants into the industry at its birth. The entire pool of potential entrants (40) jumps into the industry as it is newly born. This rush quickly slows down and the industry settles into a steady state where recurring waves

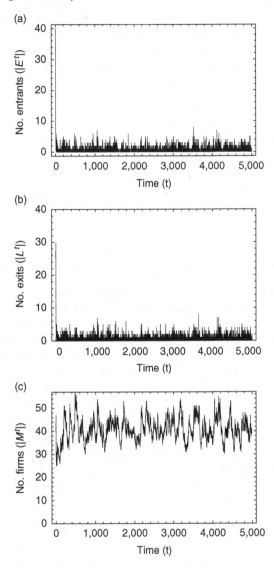

Figure 4.1 Time series of endogenous turnovers from a single replication. (a) Number of entrants, (b) Number of exiting firms, (c) Total number of firms

of new entrants are observed over the horizon. The number of exits in Figure 4.1(b) shows that the initial surge in entry is immediately followed by a large number of exits, implying that a large number of firms which initially entered the industry are soon forced out through a severe

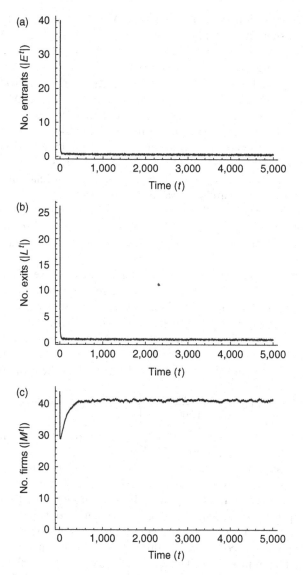

Figure 4.2 Mean time series of endogenous turnovers from 500 independent replications. (a) Number of entrants, (b) Number of exiting firms, (c) Total number of firms

market competition – i.e., a "shakeout." After the initial shakeout, the industry experiences steady out-flow of firms that accompanies the steady in-flow of firms exhibited in Figure 4.1(a). Hence, we observe *persistent* positive levels of entry and exit.

The continual streams of entries and exits interact to produce the time series in Figure 4.1(c) of the total number of firms, $|M^t|$, which includes both active and inactive firms. The time path shows that the number of firms moves with substantial volatility over time, though it moves around a steady moving average $(\cong 41)$ after about $t = 1,000$. This suggests a positive correlation between the time series of $|E^t|$ and $|L^t|$. For the baseline run reported in Figure 4.1, the correlation between the *numbers* of entry and exit was 0.58, while that between the *rates* of entry and exit was 0.57. The positive correlation between the numbers (rates) of entries and exits holds for all other runs tried in this study. The co-movement of entry and exit rates is discussed in greater detail in Chapter 5.

The time paths captured in Figure 4.1 are representative of all replications performed in this study. For multiple replications using the same baseline parameter values but with fresh random numbers (which determine the starting technologies and periodic shocks), the distribution of the period-specific outcomes generated from the stochastic process tends to be time-invariant for $t > 1,000$. Figure 4.2 shows the time series outputs of the same variables as in Figure 4.1 as the mean over 500

independent replications: $\left\{ \dfrac{1}{500} \displaystyle\sum_{k=1}^{500} X_k^t \right\}_{t=1}^{5000}$, where X_k^t is the value of the

endogenous variable X at t in replication k. As expected, the number of firms on average attains a stable level by $t = 1,000$.

Further support for the convergence to a steady state is provided in Figure 4.3 which shows the time series plots of other endogenous variables: a) market price (P^t); b) industry marginal cost (WMC^t); c) industry price-cost margin (PCM^t); d) aggregate profits (Π^t). The time paths of interest always reach a steady state by $t = 3,000$ for all parameter configurations considered in this study. As such, when we examine the impact of industry-specific factors on the industry's performance in Chapters 5–7, the steady-state value of an endogenous variable will be computed as an average over the last 2,000 periods between $t = 3,001$ and $t = 5,000$.[2]

Finally, Figure 4.4 shows the evolving degree of technological diversity (DIV^t) and the market share inequality (G^t) over time. The time series from a single replication is captured in (a) and (c), while those as an

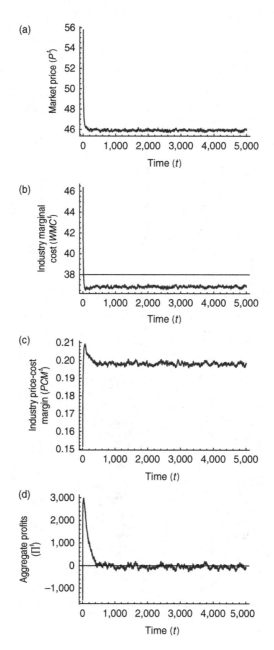

Figure 4.3 Mean time series of endogenous performance variables from 500 independent replications. (a) Market price, (b) Industry marginal cost, (c) Industry price-cost margin, (d) Aggregate profit

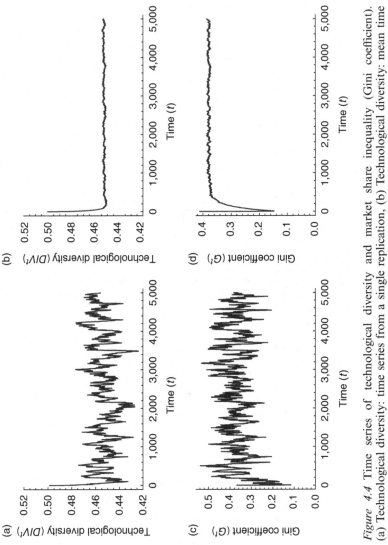

Figure 4.4 Time series of technological diversity and market share inequality (Gini coefficient). (a) Technological diversity: time series from a single replication, (b) Technological diversity: mean time series from 500 independent replications, (c) Market share inequality: time series from a single replication, (d) Market share inequality: mean time series from 500 independent replications

average over 500 independent replications are presented in (b) and (d), respectively for the two variables.

The degree of technological diversity starts at about 0.5 in the beginning, but rapidly declines to approach the steady-state mean of about 0.45. The steady state is clearly reached by $t = 1,000$. The market share inequality, as measured by the Gini coefficient, takes a severe dip during the first wave of shakeouts immediately following the birth of the industry; but it soon climbs back up to a stable level ($\cong 0.38$) as the industry converges to a steady state.

Notes

* The quote is frequently attributed to D'Arcy Thompson in his book, *On Growth and Form*. At the time of my manuscript submission, I made the same attribution with the belief that it was part of the book. When I looked for a page reference at the request of the copy editor, Miss Penny Harper, I could not find it. My limited investigation revealed that the attribution may not be accurate. The two editions of the book I had access to, the second edition (1942) from Cambridge University Press and the abridged edition (1961) edited by John Tyler Bonner, did not contain the sentence. An extensive text search of the web-based digitized versions of the first edition (1917) and the second edition (1942), using the Optical Character Recognition (OCR) software, also revealed that the oft-quoted sentence is absent. (Professor Cosma Shalizi of Carnegie Mellon, whom I had contacted in the process, had done his own independent search and came to the same conclusion.) As a last resort, I contacted Mr. Matthew Jarron, the Curator of the Museum Services at University of Dundee (where D'Arcy Thompson was the Professor of Biology for 32 years between 1884 and 1917), inquiring about the source of the quote. His email response confirmed my suspicion:

> You're absolutely right – the quote is not in either the first or second edition of *On Growth and Form* and I think it probably is not by D'Arcy, though it is often attributed to him – it's a bit too simple to match his usual style of writing. It may be that someone else was distilling his ideas and came up with that, but I'm not sure who, I'm afraid.
>
> [Email message dated September 9, 2014]

I have been unable to find the original source. In any case, the quote is so contextually appropriate for my work in this chapter that I wish I had originated it.

1 The source code for the computational experiments was written in C++ and the simulation outputs were analyzed and visualized using Mathematica 7.0. The source code is available upon request from the author.

2 See Law and Kelton (2000) for a detailed discussion of how to identify the steady state in stochastic processes. Chapter 9 on "Output Data Analysis for a Single System" is particularly useful.

5 Shakeouts

Limited foresight, technological shocks, and transient industry dynamics

It's tough to make predictions, especially about the future.
[attributed to Yogi Berra (and Niels Bohr)]

Change of some kind is prerequisite to the existence of uncertainty; in an absolutely unchanging world the future would be accurately foreknown, since it would be exactly like the past. ... It is a commonplace fact that one of the chief sources of uncertainty in business life is the improvement of technological processes, methods of organization, and the like.
[Knight (1921), pp. 313–339]

The baseline model offers results on the initial periods of high entry and exit in a new industry which closely resembles the experience of many actual industries. In this chapter I look at some of the histories, discuss some previous attempts at explanation, and compare the baseline model's results to these real histories.

It is well-known that the market histories of many manufacturing and service industries in their infancy display what is commonly known as a "shakeout." The phenomenon refers to the rapid rise in the number of producers at the opening of the new market, followed by a sharp decline (a *shakeout*), then an eventual convergence to a stable structure. The US automobile industry in its early years offers one of the more striking examples. Using the year 1895 as the founding year for the industry, Smith (1968) traces the growth and development of the industry from 1895 to 1966. He conveys in the following passage the degree of initial optimism held by the individual producers but also the general concern for the extent of its excess:

By 1905, with the decade half over, 183 new companies had undertaken the building of pleasure cars (the term then used to designate passenger cars) and 93 companies had ceased production. ... The situation was precarious with so many entering the business and sales so hard to make, and E. H. Cutler, president of the Knox Automobile Co. in Springfield, Massachusetts, was voicing the concern of many when he said: "There will be a danger from the attempt to manufacture and sell large quantities of machines that have not been fully tested; and there is a limit to the quantity that this or any other country can absorb, and we are inclined to advise conservatism in the planning of production." No one heeded this warning, no one applied brakes, and by the end of the decade 531 companies had been formed (more than one a week for ten years) and 346 had gone out of business, most through bankruptcy.

[Smith (1968), p. 25]

To see this more systematically, I plot in Figure 5.1 the number of passenger car companies in the US between 1895 and 1966 based on the data compiled by Smith (1968).[1] Figure 5.2 plots both the number of entering companies and that of exiting companies over the same time period. While the shakeout pattern is unmistakable in Figure 5.1, the entry/exit data in Figure 5.2 also indicate that the entry and exit of firms tend to occur simultaneously – a pattern that is hard to explain using the standard textbook economic theory in which the existence of economic profits invites entry while the existence of economic losses promotes exit, but never both at the same time. This general pattern also implies a substantial degree of *infant mortality*, which is captured in Figure 5.3. It plots the proportion of all exiting firms (over 1895–1966) that, at the time of exit, were of age younger than or equal to AGE (indicated along the horizontal axis). It is significant that almost 90 percent of those who exited were ten years of age or younger.

The body of scholarly work addressing the phenomenon of shakeout is not large. Gort and Klepper (1982) was the first to offer a systematic study of the shakeout phenomenon by tracing the market histories of 46 new products, identifying a distinct sequence of stages observed in the development of various industries from their birth to maturity. The findings were further elaborated upon by Klepper and Simons (1997, 2000a, 2000b), and Klepper (2002). Carroll and Hannan (2000) offered additional empirical evidence of the shakeout phenomenon in their comprehensive study of corporate demography.

There are two papers that offered stylized theoretical models capable of generating the shakeout patterns: Klepper and Graddy (1990) and Jovanovic and MacDonald (1994). Central to Klepper and Graddy's (1990) model is a group of heterogeneous potential entrants, which

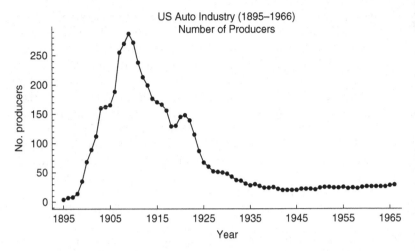

Figure 5.1 Number of producers in US automobile industry between 1895 and 1966
Source: Data: Smith (1968)

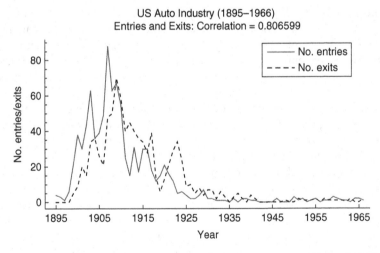

Figure 5.2 Entries and exits in US automobile industry between 1895 and 1966
Source: Data: Smith (1968)

differ from one another in terms of their costs and product qualities. They have perfect foresight and, as such, make their entry decisions on the basis of the expected discounted profits. Given the heterogeneity in their costs and product qualities, only a small number of the potential entrants actually enter the industry. The incumbent firms are

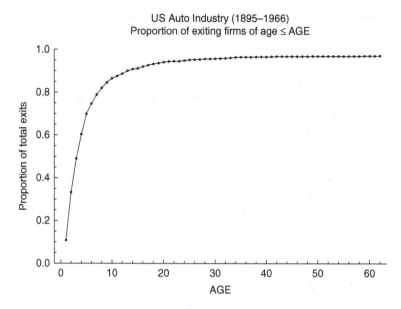

Figure 5.3 Proportion of firms exiting the US automobile industry between 1895 and 1966 that were of a given age (AGE) or younger
Source: Data: Smith (1968)

also heterogeneous in their costs and product qualities, where these differentials tend to persist because of the imperfection in the imitation activities of the firms. The shakeout pattern is then generated through the randomness in the firms' cost draws, the improvements of the cost positions through one-time imitation upon entry, and the eventual exits of those with cost positions that remain above the falling market price even after the initial improvement. Jovanovic and MacDonald (1994), using a similar conceptual framework, models the process of market competition as one in which one major invention is followed by a one-time refinement of the technology. The model is then estimated using data from the US automobile tire industry.

It is notable that both Klepper and Graddy (1990) and Jovanovic and MacDonald (1994) were able to generate the shakeout pattern using purely analytical models. However, there are two reasons why I find these models less than satisfactory. First, both models focus strictly on generating the shakeout during the *infant phase* of an industry; there are no persistent entries and exits in the long run. Hence, the scope of analysis rendered by these models tends to be rather limited. Second, both of these models employ the standard assumption of a firm as the maximizer of expected profits with perfect foresight. As discussed earlier, the environment under study is one in which there exists a great deal of uncertainty, subject to external shocks to the technological environment, perpetual innovation, imperfect imitation, and constant threats of entry by outside firms. Given the inherent randomness in this process, it is difficult to accept, on conceptual grounds, the assumption of perfect rationality and foresight.

The computational model of industry dynamics presented in this book not only allows us to replicate the stylized facts on shakeouts, but also enables comparative dynamics analysis through which we can attain the insights into how industry-specific factors influence the duration and intensity of such shakeouts. Of course, my model not only addresses the shakeout phenomena of the infant industry but allows a characterization of a mature industry as well.

5.1 Shakeout in an infant industry

5.1.1 The baseline

For purposes of evaluating the baseline model's ability to simulate a real industry, I look at a case closely related to the automobile industry. Jovanovic and MacDonald (1994) provides a clean dataset on the shakeout phenomenon in the US automobile tire industry. Using their data, I plot in Figure 5.4 the following: (a) the number of producers over 68 years from 1906 to 1973, (b) the wholesale price index over 61 years from 1913 to 1973, and (c) the industry output over 64 years from 1910 to 1973. As expected, the number of producers rises sharply in the beginning, reaching the maximum of 275 in 1922. It then declines sharply, eventually leveling off to a stable level. The wholesale price index declines over time, while the industry output rises steadily.

Given the empirical regularities presented in Figure 5.4, I now present the time series values of the relevant variables from a single sample run of my computational model, where the technological optimum is specified once in the beginning and stays fixed over the entire horizon – i.e., $\gamma = 0$. Other parameter values are set at the baseline levels indicated in Table 4.1. Assuming a stable technological environment allows us to isolate the shakeout at the infancy of the industry, thus enabling clear identification of the forces that give rise to such a phenomenon.

Figure 5.5 shows the time paths of the three variables from a single typical replication: (a) the total number of firms $(|M^t|)$; (b) the market price (P^t); and (c) the aggregate output of the industry (Q^t). These time paths are plotted only for the first 68 periods to facilitate comparisons with the empirical data plotted in Figure 5.4.

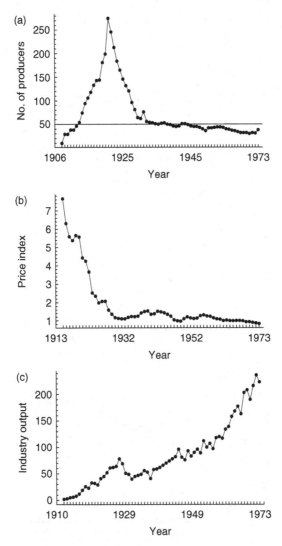

Figure 5.4 Turnover in US automobile tire industry. (a) Number of producers of automobile tires, (b) Wholesale price index for automobile tires, (c) Aggregate output
Source: Data: Jovanovic and MacDonald (1994)

The qualitative similarities between Figure 5.4 and Figure 5.5 are striking. The number of firms in the computationally generated industry shoots up in the beginning when all potential entrants decide to enter. As many of these early entrants immediately exit the industry, the

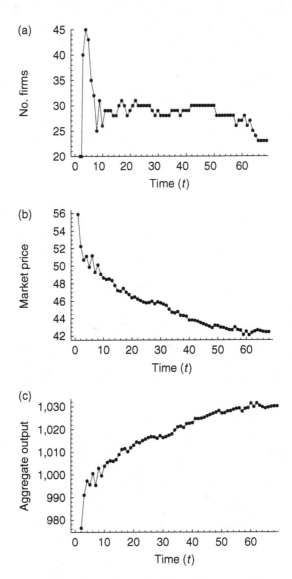

Figure 5.5 Baseline computational results from a single replication over the Jovanovic-MacDonald time span. (a) Number of firms, (b) Market price, (c) Aggregate output

number of firms sharply drops down to a relatively stable level where it fluctuates around 28 firms per period. The market price starts out high in the beginning, but drops down gradually over time, while the aggregate output tends to rise over time. The behaviors of all three variables are consistent with those reported in Figure 5.4.

Figure 5.6 shows that the shakeout phenomenon captured in Figure 5.5 is not just restricted to the single replication. For a select group of endogenous variables, it plots their time series as averages over 500 independent replications (i.e., each replication using the same baseline parameter values but a fresh set of random numbers). In order to focus on the early stage where shakeout occurs, I plot the time series on a log-linear format. Again, the number of entrants is high at the birth of the industry and declines monotonically over time. The number of exits is also high and immediately follows the movement of entries, but it also tends to decline after the initial stage. The number of firms $(|M^t|)$ in (c) displays the shakeout pattern as expected. The measure of industry concentration (HHI), H^t, dips in the beginning during the shakeout but rises gradually over time. The aggregate output (Q^t) increases and the market price (P^t) declines over time. Additionally, the industry marginal cost (WMC^t) declines monotonically, as shown in (g): Throughout the process of shakeout, the selective force of market competition pushes out the inefficient firms and permits the survival of only those with sufficiently low marginal costs. As new entrants come in with even lower marginal costs, the industry marginal cost continues to decline. While both the market price and the marginal costs decline over time, the rise in the industry price-cost margin (PCM^t), as shown in (h), indicates that the latter effect tends to dominate.

Finally, Figure 5.7 shows that the degree of technological diversity (DIV^t) and the market share inequality (G^t) both decline over time.[2] In the context of our model, this is consistent with the monotonically declining industry marginal cost in Figure 5.6(g). As more efficient firms are selected through market competition, these firms tend to have technologies that are closer to the (fixed) technological optimum and thus are closer to one another in the technology space; hence the uniform decline in technological diversity in (a). The technological convergence also implies that the market shares of the firms are increasingly equalized over time, as shown in (b). In the absence of external shocks to the technological environment, the degree of technological diversity and the market share inequality both converge to zero in the long run.

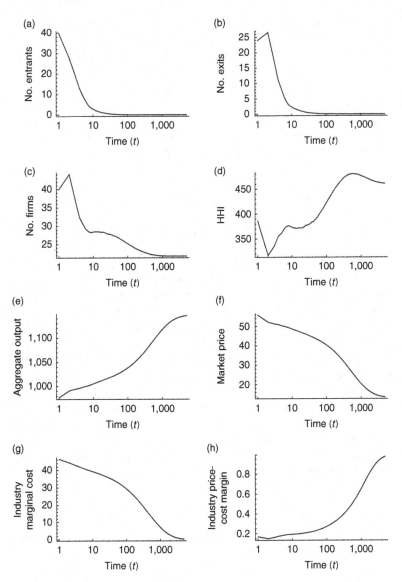

Figure 5.6 Mean time series of endogenous variables from 500 independent replications. (a) Number of entrants, (b) Number of exiting firms, (c) Number of firms, (d) Industry concentration, (e) Aggregate output, (f) Market price, (g) Industry marginal cost, (h) Industry price-cost margin

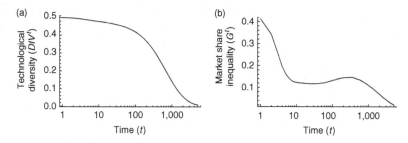

Figure 5.7 Mean time series of technological diversity and market share inequality from 500 independent replications. (a) Technological diversity, (b) Market share inequality

5.1.2 Comparative dynamics

Given that the shakeout is an essential part of an industry in its early phase, a relevant question is how the severity of the shakeout is affected by the industry-specific factors. In fact, I focus here on the impact that two structural parameters, f and s, have on the time paths of the relevant endogenous variables.

I first consider four different values of the fixed cost, $f \in \{200, 300, 400, 500\}$, while holding the market size constant at $s = 4$. The time series of the mean over 500 replications are reported in Figures 5.8 through 5.10. Similarly, I consider $s \in \{3, 4, 5, 6\}$, while holding f fixed at the baseline value of 200, and report the corresponding results in Figures 5.11 through 5.13.

Figure 5.8(a) and (b) show respectively that the number of entrants and the number of exits are both higher for higher fixed cost during the shakeout phase. The main driver of this property is the bounded rationality assumed for our potential entrants. A potential entrant in this model makes its entry decision under the assumption that it is the only new entrant into the market. When the size of the fixed cost is larger, the cost of making the cognitive error is higher (bigger losses). This leads to the number of active firms being lower and the number of inactive firms being higher. As the entry decision in any given period is based on the surviving firms that were active in the previous period, the fact that there is a lesser number of active firms implies the potential entrants are more likely to enter (and make the costly error) when the fixed cost is larger. Of course, the higher cost of making the error implies more firms exiting each period during the initial phase of the shakeout. The shakeout is clearly more severe when the fixed cost is higher.

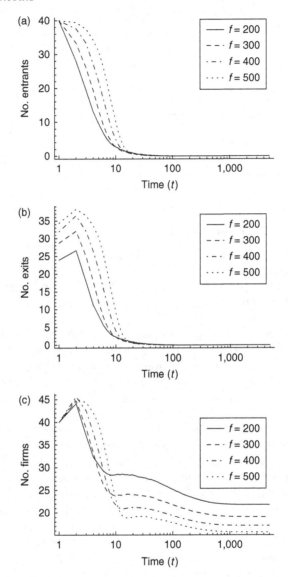

Figure 5.8 Impact of fixed cost (*f*) on shakeout. (a) Number of entrants, (b) Number of exits, (c) Number of firms

The total number of firms, shown in Figure 5.8(c), includes both active and inactive firms and is initially higher for higher fixed cost, but *in the long run* the industry with a higher fixed cost can only sustain a smaller number of firms (as inactive firms must eventually exit

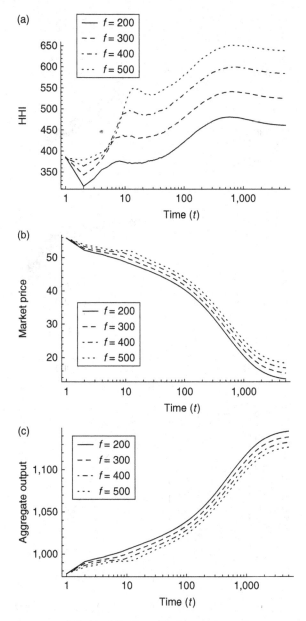

Figure 5.9 Impact of fixed cost (*f*) on shakeout. (a) Industry concentration, (b) Market price, (c) Aggregate output

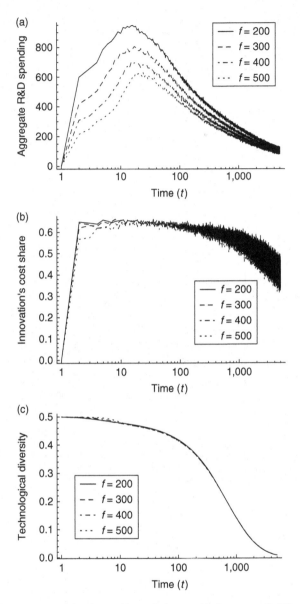

Figure 5.10 Impact of fixed cost (*f*) on shakeout. (a) Aggregate R&D spending, (b) Innovation's share of R&D spending, (c) Technological diversity

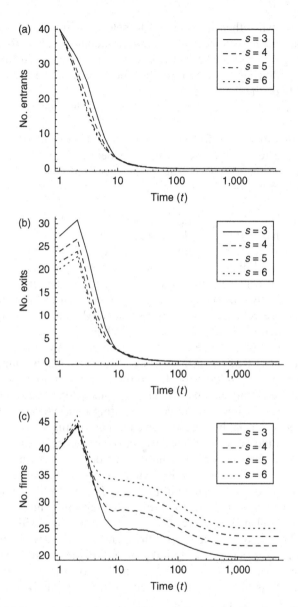

Figure 5.11 Impact of market size (*s*) on shakeout. (a) Number of entrants, (b) Number of exits, (c) Number of firms

the industry when their net wealth falls below the threshold level). This gives us a shakeout process that is more gradual but also more severe in the long run. Given the focus on the shakeout phase in the beginning, the following property describes the impact of the fixed cost on the severity of the shakeout.

Property 5.1: The shakeout is more severe for an industry with higher fixed costs.

The structure and performance of the industry during the shakeout are also affected by the fixed cost. As expected, Figure 5.9(a) shows the industry is more concentrated when its fixed cost is higher. The higher concentration leads to higher market price and lower aggregate output.

Finally, Figure 5.10 shows that the aggregate R&D spending (TRD^t) during the shakeout phase is lower when the fixed cost is higher, but the share of innovation in the total R&D spending (NRD^t) and the degree of technological diversity appear not very sensitive to the size of the fixed cost. The negative impact the fixed cost has on the aggregate R&D spending is likely due to there being fewer (active) firms in the industry when the fixed cost is higher. It is also worthwhile to note that NRD^t starts out high at about 0.6, but then declines over time:[3] Innovative R&D is dominant in the beginning, but then gradually loses its dominance to imitative R&D over time. The decline in the relative importance of innovation over imitation is due to the assumption that the technological environment remains perfectly stationary for these simulations. Given the fixed optimum technology, imitating a more successful rival is likely to be increasingly more effective than innovating by oneself. This tendency should be reduced once we introduce recurrent shocks to the technological environment. The monotonic decline over time of DIV^t for all values of f, as captured in Figure 5.10(c), is as expected.

Similar results are presented in Figures 5.11–5.13 for different values of the market size, s. Both the number of entrants and the number of exits are higher during the shakeout for an industry with a smaller market. The resulting number of firms in the industry, as shown in Figure 5.11(c), seems relatively independent of the market size during the shakeout period, but is uniformly higher for a larger market size afterwards, thus confirming the capacity of the larger market to sustain a greater number of firms in the long run.

Property 5.2: The shakeout is more severe in smaller markets.

Figure 5.12 shows that a smaller market is naturally more concentrated with the consequence of a higher market price and a lower aggregate output. Figure 5.13 shows that the aggregate R&D spending is higher in larger markets (again likely due to there being more firms in

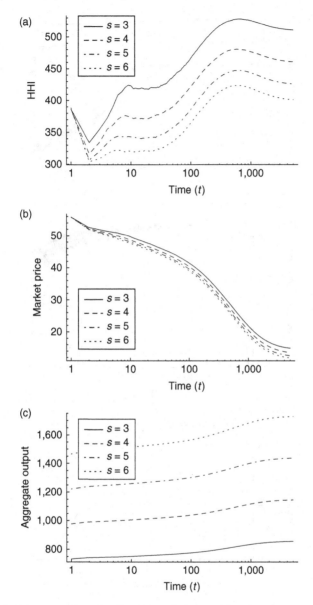

Figure 5.12 Impact of market size (*s*) on shakeout. (a) Industry concentration, (b) Market price, (c) Aggregate output

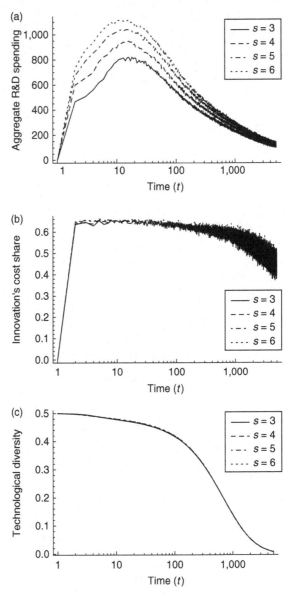

Figure 5.13 Impact of market size (*s*) on shakeout. (a) Aggregate R&D spending, (b) Innovation's share of R&D spending, (c) Technological diversity

larger markets); hence, one expects more intense R&D during a shake-out when the industry faces a larger market demand. The innovation's share of R&D cost and the degree of technological diversity, as in the case of fixed cost, are unaffected by the size of the market demand. It should also be noted that the declining trends in the time series of the two endogenous variables are present for all market sizes considered here, just as in Figure 5.10 for the case of different fixed costs.

Although the results in this section are limited to a special case designed for studying the shakeout behavior during the infancy of an industry, they do indicate that the market size (s) and the fixed cost (f) have opposite effects on the variables describing the behavior of the industry. The comparative dynamics analysis performed in the next chapter shows that this is indeed the case more generally.

5.2 Technological change and recurrent shakeouts

In Section 5.1, I focused on the shakeout in an infant industry by keep-ing the technological optimum fixed throughout the entire horizon. More generally, the technological environment is likely to be subject to recurring shocks. In this model, the *persistence* of firm entries and exits over time comes from the unexpected shifts in the technological envir-onment surrounding the firms (which happens at the rate of γ, where $\gamma = 0.1$ for the baseline case). To verify the relevance of this mechanism, I track the occurrences of technological shifts over the entire horizon. For a given technological shift that occurs in period τ, I define its "epi-sode" as those consecutive periods following the shift before the next technological shift occurs in period τ'. The duration of the episode is then ($\tau'-\tau$).

For the baseline run captured in Figure 4.1, there were 504 (completed) episodes of varying durations over the entire horizon of 5,000 periods. This number of episodes is as expected, given the rate of technological change at $\gamma = 0.1$.[4] The durations of the episodes, however, are quite variable. Figure 5.14 shows how many times an episode of a given dur-ation appeared over the time periods between $t = 1,001$ and 5,000 – the first 1,000 periods are excluded because of their transient nature. Over these 4,000 periods the longest episode had the duration of 66 (there was one such episode), while the shortest episode lasted only 1 period (there were 45 of them).

Figure 5.15 plots each episode in terms of its duration (along the horizontal axis) and its size (along the vertical axis) as measured by the total number of entries (a) and by the total number of exits (b) that occurred during the episode. As expected, they are highly correlated:

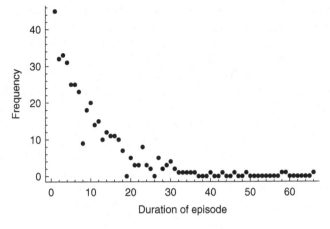

Figure 5.14 Frequency of various durations of episodes from a single replication

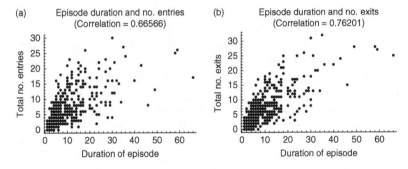

Figure 5.15 Duration of episodes and the size of firm movements. (a) Total number of entries, (b) Total number of exits

An episode of longer duration tends to entail greater number of entries and exits.

To see the impact that technological shifts have on the turnover of firms in greater detail, I now ask, for each period over the horizon ($1,001 \leq t \leq 5,000$), how many periods have elapsed since the last technological shift. This allows me to examine the relationship between the rates of entry and exit and the elapsed time since a technological shift. Figure 5.16(a) and Figure 5.16(b) capture this information. On average, both rates tend to fall as the given period is further away from the last technological shift. (The correlations between the rates and the

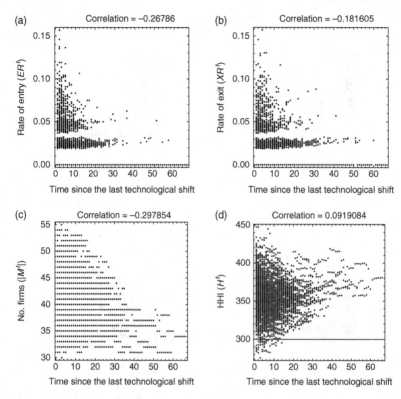

Figure 5.16 Relationship between the endogenous variables and the time since the last technological shift. (a) Rate of entry, (b) Rate of exit, (c) Number of firms, (d) Industry concentration

time since the last technological shock are noted on the corresponding figures.) The total number of firms (Figure 5.16(c)) is also negatively correlated with the time since the last technological shift, even though the industry concentration (HHI) in Figure 5.16(d) shows a very weak positive correlation.

These correlations indicate that the relationships between these turn-over variables and the time since the last technological shock are similar in nature to those identified in the case of shakeouts in infant industries with no technological shocks. In the presence of recurrent technological shifts, one may then view the turnover dynamics as being a series of *mini-shakeouts*, in which the rates of entry and exit jump up immediately following a technological shift and then gradually fall down as the market adjusts to the new environment. The persistent series of entries

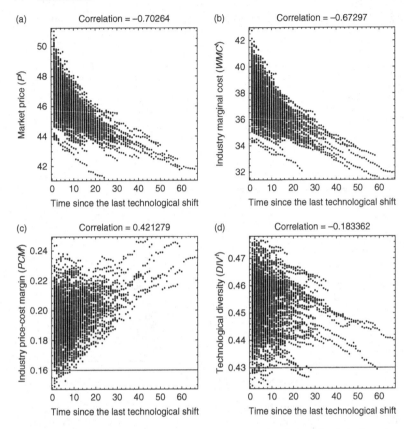

Figure 5.17 Relationship between the endogenous variables and the time since the last technological shift. (a) Market price, (b) Industry marginal cost, (c) Industry price-cost margin, (d) Technological diversity

and exits over time, as well as the positive correlation between the time series of the corresponding rates, are then a natural consequence of these repeated shakeouts following technological shifts.

The recurring shakeouts also display noticeable patterns in other endogenous variables; these patterns are consistent with those identified in the infant industries. Figure 5.17(a) shows that the market price is significantly negatively correlated with the time since the last technological shift. As previously shown, this is due to the drop in the marginal costs resulting from the market selection. The industry marginal cost is also negatively correlated with the time since the last technological shift – see Figure 5.17(b). Industry price-cost margin is positively correlated with the shift, while the degree of technological diversity is negatively (though weakly) correlated.

Notes

1 The original list compiled by Smith (1968) – referred to as "basic list A" – contains all "makes" of passenger cars produced commercially in the United States from 1895 to 1966 along with their years of production. The year of entry for a company is hence represented by the year production commenced, while the year of exit is represented by the year production ceased. The list was converted into a manageable dataset by Endrit Meta.
2 Technological diversity declines monotonically throughout the entire horizon. The market share inequality, while also showing a general decline over time, displays a slight break in the earlier part of the horizon between $t = 30$ and $t = 200$.
3 It should be noted that the new entrants do not perform R&D during the period of their entry. This explains why both TRD^t and NRD^t in Figure 5.10. (a)–(b) start at zero in $t = 1$ when every firm is a new entrant.
4 With $\gamma = 0.1$, a new episode is expected every ten periods. Hence, a total of about 500 episodes should be expected over the horizon of 5,000 periods.

6 Industry dynamics in the steady state

Between-industry variations

> Inter-industry research has taught us much about how markets look, especially within the manufacturing sector in developed economies, even if it has not shown us exactly how markets work.
>
> [Schmalensee (1989), p. 1000]

The baseline analysis in Chapter 4 indicated that, even with the persistent shocks to the firms' technological environment, the industry eventually reaches a steady state in which a typical endogenous variable fluctuates around a constant mean. However, the shakeout analysis in Chapter 5 also indicated that even within the steady state there are systematic patterns across time as the result of external shocks to the technological environment. In this chapter, I pursue two objectives: 1) to identify and explain the temporal patterns at the aggregate industry level that exist along the steady-state path; and 2) to perform a comparative dynamics analysis of the steady state with respect to the two parameters, the size of the market (s) and the fixed cost (f), which represent the factors specific to an industry.

The empirical relevance of the comparative study of steady states presented in this chapter can be seen in the observed variation in entry and exit patterns across industries as reported in Dunne, Roberts, and Samuelson (1988) (DRS (1988) from here on). I plot in Figure 6.1 the summary measures of the entry and exit patterns across industries obtained from DRS (1988). Specifically, DRS (1988) average the rate of entry and the rate of exit over the four time-period observations for the four-digit SIC industries from their sample.[1] Grouping the four-digit industries into 20 two-digit sectors, they then report the distributions of these average rates for each sector. In Figure 6.1 I plot the sector-averages of these rates for all 20 sectors in their study, where the horizontal coordinate and the vertical coordinate of a given point (sector) capture

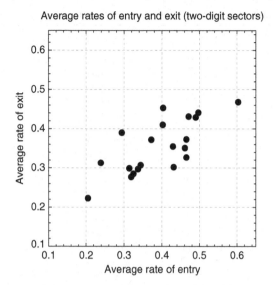

Figure 6.1 Average rate of entry and average rate of exit across 20 two-digit sectors
Source: Data: DRS (1988)

the average rate of entry and the average rate of exit, respectively, for the sector.

The way these points are dispersed along the diagonal makes it quite clear that the rate of entry and the rate of exit are positively correlated (at 0.732) across all sectors: A sector with a higher (lower) than average rate of entry also tends to have a higher (lower) than average rate of exit. For instance, the Instruments sector (SIC 38) has the highest rate of entry (0.603) as well as the highest rate of exit (0.468) in this sample, while the Tobacco sector (SIC 21) has the lowest rate of entry (0.205) and the lowest rate of exit (0.223). Hence, the industries vary in terms of the severity of turnovers. The comparative dynamics analysis carried out in this chapter will show that our model indeed generates this type of diversity along the steady state of the stochastic process and enables us to identify the causal relationships between the underlying parameters and these variations.

6.1 Defining the steady state

I start by providing a precise description of the process through which I study the steady state. For a given parameter configuration, I perform 500 independent replications, using fresh sequence of random numbers

Table 6.1 Steady-state means of the endogenous variables*

Variable	Mean	Standard deviation
$|E^t|$	0.684	0.0606
$|L^t|$	0.683	0.0606
$|M^t|$	41.170	0.4837
ER^t	0.016	0.0015
XR^t	0.016	0.0015
P^t	45.924	0.2108
Q^t	1,016.300	0.8433
Π^t	−53.840	113.4550
PCM^t	0.198	0.0019
WMC^t	36.842	0.2335
H^t	357.458	2.6171
TRD^t	1,051.320	17.2790
NRD^t	0.644	0.0025
CS^t	129,114.000	214.6020
TS^t	129,060.000	261.6590
DIV^t	0.453	0.0027
G^t	0.379	0.0091

*These are the descriptive statistics of the steady-state means from the 500 independent replications. Each steady-state mean is the average over the 2,000 periods between $t = 3,001$ and $5,000$.

for each replication. The time series values of the endogenous variables are collected for the last 2,000 periods from $t = 3,001$ to $t = 5,000$. These time series characterize the steady-state paths of these endogenous variables.

Suppose a given replication k generates time series values for an endogenous variable X as $\left\{X_k^t\right\}_{t=1}^{5,000}$, where X_k^t is the value of X in period t from replication k. The steady-state mean of X for the given replication k is denoted $\bar{X}_k$, where $\bar{X}_k = \dfrac{1}{2,000} \sum_{t=3,001}^{5,000} X_k^t$. For each endogenous variable, X, there will be 500 steady-state means (from 500 independent replications), $\left\{\bar{X}_k\right\}_{k=1}^{500}$. The mean and the standard deviation of these 500 steady-state means, generated under the baseline parameter configuration, are reported in Table 6.1. It is notable that the aggregate profit, Π^t, is negative on average. This reflects the significant economic losses taken by the *inactive* firms which are not currently in operation (though still paying for the fixed costs). These firms linger on as long as their accumulated net wealth exceeds the threshold level that reflects the opportunity cost of their resources.

When performing the comparative dynamics analysis, the average behavior of the industry with respect to a given endogenous variable X is represented by averaging $\bar{X}_k$ over all replications: $\bar{X} = \dfrac{1}{500}\displaystyle\sum_{k=1}^{500}\bar{X}_k$.

6.2 Temporal patterns along the steady state within an industry

Recall from Chapter 5 that the long-run dynamics of the firms can be understood as recurrent shakeouts in the presence of persistent changes in the technological environment. A logical implication of that perspective was the correlated movement of firms in and out of the market, which also had implications for the performance of firms and the industry over time. To confirm the presence and the significance of the relationships between the endogenous variables, I report in Table 6.2 the correlations between the steady-state time series of all relevant pairs of the endogenous variables, X and Y, over the steady state. The value in each cell is the average of these correlations from 500 independent replications: $\bar{\rho}_{XY} = \dfrac{1}{500}\displaystyle\sum_{k=1}^{500}\mathrm{Corr}[\{X_k^t\}_{t=3,001}^{5,000}, \{Y_k^t\}_{t=3,001}^{5,000}]$.

To begin, the rates of entry and exit, ER^t and XR^t, are positively correlated at 0.321. Although not included in the table, the *number* of entries, $|E^t|$, and the *number* of exits, $|L^t|$, are also positively correlated with the mean value of 0.371.

Property 6.1: The rate of entry and the rate of exit are positively correlated over time: When the rate of entry is high (low), the rate of exit is also high (low).

This result is consistent with the third stylized fact mentioned in Chapter 1. Of course, this stylized fact is at odds with the standard textbook view that the presence of economic profits induces entry and that of economic losses induces exit (which implies a negative correlation between the rate of entry and the rate of exit over time). Commenting on the discrepancy between the accepted view and the empirical findings, Geroski (1995, p. 424) observes:

> This view is difficult to reconcile with the fact that a typical three digit industry in UK gained an average of 50 new firms *per year* over the period 1974–1979 and lost an average of 38, experiencing a net entry rate of just over 1% and a negative net penetration rate of −0.42%.

Table 6.2 Correlations between endogenous variables (average over 500 independent replications)

	ER^t	XR^t	$|M^t|$	P^t	Q^t	Π^t	PCM^t	WMC^t	H^t	TRD^t	NRD^t	CS^t	TS^t	DIV^t	G^t
ER^t	1														
XR^t	0.321	1													
$|M^t|$	0.262	0.264	1												
P^t	0.318	0.208	0.340	1											
Q^t	−0.318	−0.208	−0.340	−1	1										
Π^t	−0.276	−0.281	−0.928	−0.337	0.337	1									
PCM^t	−0.329	−0.260	−0.632	−0.530	0.530	0.831	1								
WMC^t	0.368	0.260	0.518	0.923	−0.923	−0.606	−0.814	1							
H^t	−0.225	−0.200	−0.565	−0.103	0.103	0.799	0.895	−0.475	1						
TRD^t	0.050	0.172	0.490	0.173	−0.173	−0.585	−0.310	0.258	−0.274	1					
NRD^t	0.003	0.003	0.018	0.011	−0.011	−0.076	−0.016	0.015	−0.012	0.344	1				
CS^t	−0.318	−0.208	−0.341	−1.000	1.000	0.338	0.530	−0.923	0.103	−0.173	−0.011	1			
TS^t	−0.362	−0.362	−0.791	−0.799	0.799	0.834	0.839	−0.926	0.569	−0.474	−0.055	0.800	1		
DIV^t	0.246	0.253	0.692	0.430	−0.430	−0.651	−0.496	0.517	−0.356	0.399	0.019	−0.431	−0.667	1	
G^t	0.140	0.162	0.787	0.345	−0.345	−0.536	−0.124	0.291	0.036	0.391	0.013	−0.345	−0.544	0.591	1

He also finds from the Canadian data during the 1970s that the rate of entry and the rate of exit averaged 5 percent and 6.5 percent, respectively, resulting in a net entry rate of −1.5 percent. These findings indicate that the arrival of a large number of new firms tends to occur together with the departure of a large number of older firms, hence, implying a positive correlation between the rates.

The co-movement of the two rates suggests that the rate of firm turnover can be described by either the rate of entry or the rate of exit (or even by the sum of the two rates as specified in some of the past empirical works). A later result on comparative dynamics indicates that the two rates are positively correlated across different industries as well. Hence, I will simply use the *rate of entry* to capture the *rate of turnover*.

As we saw in Chapter 5, the positive correlation between the time series of the rate of entry and the rate of exit can be understood in the context of "recurrent shakeouts" in the presence of external technological shocks. Geroski (1995) offers an insightful discussion that supports this perspective. After stating that "Entry rates vary over time, coming in waves which often peak early in the life of many markets. Different waves tend to contain different types of entrant," he observes:

> [A]t least two generations of entrant appeared in the US computer industry … the first were major business machine firms whose existing activities were threatened by the new technology (e.g. IBM, Remington, NCR, Burroughs), while the second were new, specialized firms interested in developing and exploiting the new technology (e.g. Philco, GE, CDC and DEC). Similarly, receiving tube producers (e.g. General Electric, RCA, Sylvania and others) were the first to colonize the US semiconductor industry, followed more slowly by other producers in the electronics sector, in-house producers and new high-tech specialists.
>
> [Geroski (1995), p. 426]

Geroski's discussion focuses on technological changes in "products," while my model addresses technological changes in the "production process." Nevertheless, the basic mechanism underlying the waves of entry is the same. It is the unexpected inventions and innovations arriving from outside the industry that affect the technological environment for the firms asymmetrically, thus inducing waves of entries and exits.

The "recurrent shakeout" perspective also implies that the price must be positively correlated with both the entry and exit rates of firms, as it is when the technological environment shifts that the incumbent firms using the old technology will suddenly find themselves inadequately prepared for the new environment. The sudden drop in the average level of efficiency (and the corresponding rise in the firms' marginal costs) leads to an increase in the market price. As firms adapt to the new environment and improve their production efficiency, the market price gradually declines while at the same time the entry and exit of firms slow down. Thus, the price, P^t, is positively correlated with the rates of entry and exit. Indeed, the mean correlations are 0.318 and 0.208, respectively.

The aggregate profit, Π^t, is negatively correlated with the entry and exit of firms. This is again due to the external shock in the technological environment adversely affecting the firms' efficiency initially; the endogenous R&D raising it back up as firms adapt themselves to the new environment. As expected, the aggregate profit is also negatively correlated with the total number of firms in the industry.

Similar to the aggregate profit, the industry price-cost margin, PCM^t, is negatively correlated with both entry and exit, as well as with the total number of firms. It is interesting to note, however, that it is negatively correlated with the market price, P^t. The shakeout perspective provides an explanation. Note that the market price is driven by the level of firms' efficiency: A high price reflects a high marginal cost (low efficiency), while a low price reflects a low marginal cost (high efficiency). Although the market price and the firms' marginal costs tend to move in the same direction, the negative relationship between P^t and PCM^t suggests that a given change in the marginal cost is likely to have a less than equal effect on the market price.

The relationships between the industry marginal cost, WMC^t, and various endogenous variables as reported in Table 6.2 are fully consistent with the shakeout-based explanations provided above. The industry marginal cost, WMC^t, is positively correlated with entry, exit, and the number of firms. It also displays a strongly positive correlation (0.923) with the market price as expected, but a strongly negative correlation (−0.814) with the price-cost margin.

The concentration measure, H^t, is negatively correlated with the number of operating firms (−0.565), while positively correlated with both the aggregate profit (0.799) and the price-cost margin (0.895): a period of higher concentration is also likely to show higher aggregate profits and a higher price-cost margin.

Property 6.2: The industry concentration is negatively correlated with the industry marginal cost over time, while it is positively correlated with the industry price-cost margin over time.

The positive correlation between the time series of industry concentration and price-cost margin would be logical in the context of oligopoly theory in which market concentration tends to raise the market power and the equilibrium firm profits. However, it is important to note that the underlying mechanism here relies less on the market power argument, but more on the efficiency effect. The external shock to the environment temporarily reduces the firms' profits through an increase in their marginal costs (i.e., loss of efficiency), while it promotes turnovers that reduce the degree of concentration. It is the adaptive moves by the firms through their R&D that reverse these changes gradually until the next technological shock. The negative correlation (-0.475) between H^t and WMC^t is consistent with this explanation.

The variable capturing the R&D intensity within the industry, TRD^t, is positively correlated with the total number of firms, $|M^t|$, while negatively correlated with the aggregate profit, Π^t, and the price-cost margin, PCM^t. The innovation's share of the R&D cost, NRD^t, does not show any noticeable correlation with other variables, though it is positively correlated with the aggregate R&D spending (TRD^t).

The negative relationships between the performance measures (i.e., aggregate profits and the price-cost margin) and the R&D spending are due to the heightened R&D activities during the periods immediately following the external shock to the technological environment. A sudden change in the technological environment, while undermining the profitability of the previously well-adapted incumbents, also offers a fresh set of opportunities for the incumbents and the potential entrants alike.

In terms of the welfare measures, the consumer surplus is negatively correlated with the firms' entry and exit activities for the obvious reason that the market price tends to be high during the period of high turnover. The consumer surplus is positively correlated with the aggregate profit and the industry price-cost margin, while negatively correlated with the industry marginal cost. It is interesting to note that the consumer surplus is negatively correlated with the aggregate R&D spending (TRD^t). The explanation lies in the fact that those periods with relatively active R&D are the ones that have recently been hit with the external shock in the technological environment and, hence, the firms are relatively inefficient and the market price tends to be high. The total surplus (TS^t) displays similar properties: It is negatively correlated with the entry/exit activities, while positively correlated with the performance variables (profits and price-cost margin). It is also negatively correlated with the aggregate R&D spending for the same reason described above for the consumer surplus.

The technological diversity (DIV^t) is positively correlated with the rates of entry and exit, as well as with the total number of firms. The external shocks to the technological environment bring about waves of entry and exit; the new entrants come in with a wide variety of new technologies. As the industry adapts to the new environment, the selective force of the market competition that weeds out the inefficient firms then leads to increased concentration and a reduction in the variety of surviving technologies; hence the negative correlation (−0.356) between DIV^t and H^t. It is also notable that the technological diversity is positively correlated with the aggregate R&D (0.399).

Finally, the Gini coefficient, which measures the inequality in the market shares of the firms, shows a mild positive correlation with the entry/ exit of firms, while it has a strongly positive correlation (0.787) with the number of firms.[2] This indicates a more unequal market share distribution during those periods when the firms are actively moving in and out of the market. As such, it is also positively correlated with technological diversity (0.591). As the firms adapt to the new environment and the industry becomes more concentrated, their technologies (and their marginal costs) tend to converge, thus leading to a more equal distribution of market shares within the industry.

6.3 Between-industry variations in steady states

While the non-equilibrium dynamics of the kind described above are common to all industries, the extent to which they affect the structure and performance of the industry along the steady-state path can differ from industry to industry. In this section, I compare the steady states of industries with different characteristics and explore the causal factors behind the observed heterogeneity.

There are four main parameters in the model that define the characteristics of an industry: the size of the market (s), the size of the fixed cost (f), the rate of change in the technological environment (γ), and the maximum magnitude of change in the technological environment (g). The latter two parameters, γ and g, describe the turbulent nature of the external technological environment. The shocks to the technological environment are assumed exogenous to the industry and thus have an external source. Because the impacts of γ and g on the adaptive dynamics of the firms are rather intuitive and straightforward, I restrict the comparative dynamics analysis to s and f for expositional simplicity.

As described earlier, the comparative analysis focuses on the steady-state means of the endogenous variables averaged over 500 independent replications for each parameter configuration that represents a particular industry. This means the average steady-state means of an endogenous variable X, denoted $\bar{X}$, is specific to a given industry characterized by a particular pair of parameter values, (s, f). The comparative dynamics analysis entails comparing the values of $\bar{X}$ for different configurations of s and f, each representing a specific type of industry. In particular, I consider $s \in \{3, 4, 5, 6\}$ and $f \in \{200, 300, 400, 500\}$.

6.3.1 Steady-state volatility of an industry

The external shocks to the technological environment induce persistent turnover of firms, generating endogenous volatility in the structure of the industry. Such structural volatility has two distinct components: 1) the fluctuation in the size and composition of the industry due to the movements of firms *in and out of the industry*; 2) the fluctuation in the distribution of market shares among firms *within the industry*. The first component characterizes the turbulence at the boundary of an industry. For expositional convenience, I will refer to it as *inter-industry volatility*. In the context of our model, the term "inter-industry" reflects the fact that a firm exiting an industry may be viewed as moving to another industry that offers the next best alternative opportunity. Similarly, a new entrant could be viewed as coming from another industry. The second component characterizes turbulence strictly within the industry, in that the focus is on the frequency with which the market dominance changes hands. It reflects the changing fortunes of the incumbent firms caused by the unexpected changes in the technological environment and the stochastic nature of their R&D activities. I will refer to this type of volatility as *intra-industry volatility*.

In my model, the inter-industry volatility is captured by the usual rates of entry and exit (turnover). The intra-industry volatility, however, is more difficult to gauge, as it involves the changing positions of all firms within the industry. In this study, I will focus on a particular aspect of that volatility; namely, the (in-)ability of the market leader – i.e., the firm with the largest market share – to retain its dominant position. There are two equivalent ways to capture this: 1) the number of consecutive periods during which a market leader stays in the leadership position (duration of the leadership); 2) the frequency with which the identity of the leader changes. The latter measure is immediate, once we have a complete record of the leadership durations over the horizon. While both measures provide the same information, the "frequency of leadership changes" will be mainly used in this section to represent the intra-industry volatility.

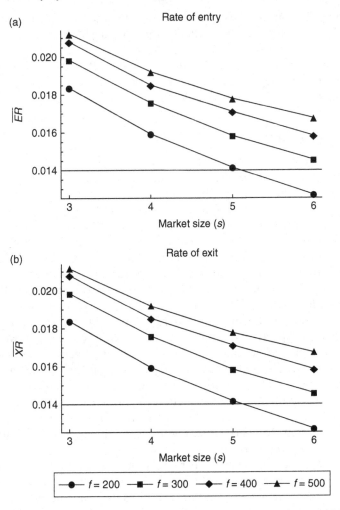

Figure 6.2 Impact of market size (*s*) and fixed cost (*f*) on firm turnover. (a) Rate of entry, (b) Rate of exit

Figure 6.2 plots the mean steady-state rates of entry and exit, $\overline{ER}$ and $\overline{XR}$, for $s \in \{3, 4, 5, 6\}$ and $f \in \{200, 300, 400, 500\}$. As displayed in the figure, both rates decrease with the size of the market (*s*) and increase with the size of the fixed cost (*f*). Hence, given a group of heterogeneous industries, differentiated in terms of the market size and fixed cost, an industry with a high (low) rate of entry is also likely to have a high (low) rate of exit; some industries exhibit inherently greater

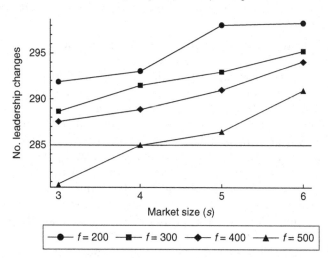

Figure 6.3 Impact of market size (*s*) and fixed cost (*f*) on intra-industry volatility (frequency of leadership changes)

inter-industry volatility than others. Specifically, an industry serving a smaller market and/or having a higher fixed cost displays a higher degree of *inter-industry volatility*.

Property 6.3: The rate of turnover (inter-industry volatility) decreases with the size of the market and increases with the size of the fixed cost.

Since the rate of entry and the rate of exit respond to the parameters in the same way (i.e., both higher or both lower), this result is fully consistent with the finding of DRS (1988) as captured in Figure 6.1: an industry with a higher (lower) rate of entry also has a higher (lower) rate of exit.

To explore the intra-industry volatility, I track the duration of the market dominance for each leader over the 2,000 periods of the steady state between $t = 3,001$ and $t = 5,000$ for each replication; only the fully completed leadership episodes (those that started after $t = 3,001$ and ended before $t = 5,000$) are counted. This exercise also gives us the number of times that the market leadership changed hands over the steady state for each replication. Taking the mean over the 500 replications, Figure 6.3 shows that the mean number of leadership changes is higher in an industry with a larger market size (*s*) and/or a smaller fixed cost (*f*).

Property 6.4: The frequency of leadership changes (intra-industry vola-tility) increases with the size of the market and decreases with the size of the fixed cost.

Equivalently, the mean duration of the leadership declines with market size (s) and increases with fixed cost (f).

Let us now consider the relationship between the inter-industry volatility and the intra-industry volatility. Notice from Property 6.3 and Property 6.4 that the inter-industry volatility (rate of turnover) and the intra-industry volatility (frequency of leadership changes) are negatively related to each other. An industry with a higher (lower) inter-industry volatility has a lower (higher) intra-industry volatility. For instance, consider two heterogeneous industries; industry A with $s = 6$ and $f = 200$ and industry B with $s = 3$ and $f = 500$. Industry A exhibits the rate of entry at about 1.25 percent but the market leadership changed about 298 times. In industry B, the rate of entry is around 2.15 percent and the market leadership changes about 281 times. Hence, industry A shows greater intra-industry volatility, but industry B shows greater inter-industry volatility.

The divergent manner in which the two types of volatility respond to the two parameters indicates that it is inadequate for understanding the underlying dynamics to describe the structural volatility of an industry using only the rate of turnover. An important question is: What drives the difference in the two volatility measures? It turns out that the answer to this question lies in the way R&D influences the selective force of the market competition.

To test the effect of R&D on the industry volatility, let us run the baseline replication under the alternative condition that the firms perform no R&D. Firms are assumed to come into the industry with a randomly chosen technology which then stays fixed for the rest of the firm's life. The entry and exit of the firms are purely driven by the selective force of the market competition, with no adaptive efforts (i.e., R&D) by the firms. We will compare the outcome from this alternative case to that from the original baseline with endogenous R&D.

Figure 6.4 reports on the results of this experiment by plotting histograms of the mean steady-state values of the four endogenous variables from the 500 independent replications of the baseline case with and without endogenous R&D: a) the rate of entry; b) the rate of exit; c) the duration of industry leadership; and d) the frequency of leadership changes. First, note that the presence of endogenous R&D shifts the rates of entry and exit downward. Hence, there is less inter-industry volatility in the presence of endogenous R&D. Second, endogenous

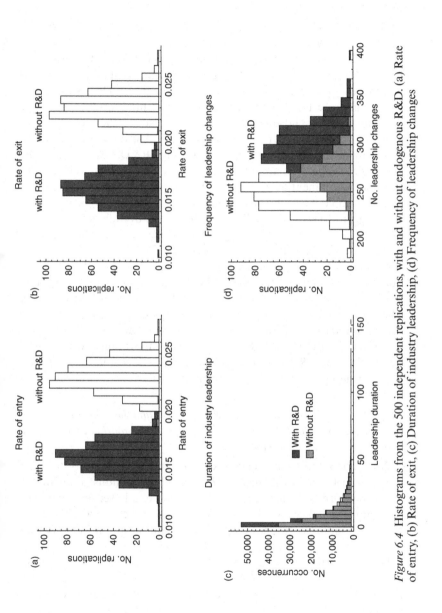

Figure 6.4 Histograms from the 500 independent replications, with and without endogenous R&D. (a) Rate of entry, (b) Rate of exit, (c) Duration of industry leadership, (d) Frequency of leadership changes

R&D shifts the leadership duration downward and the frequency of leadership changes upward: there is greater intra-industry volatility in the presence of endogenous R&D.

Property 6.5: Endogenous R&D reduces inter-industry volatility, but increases intra-industry volatility.

Clearly, the pursuit of R&D by firms allows the incumbents to adapt to the changing environment to a greater extent, compared to the situation where they have no such adaptation mechanism. The resulting cost advantage protects the incumbents from the potential entrants who come in with randomly chosen technologies; this leads to the reduced inter-industry volatility under endogenous R&D.[3] However, the improved efficiency of the incumbents, attained through R&D, also increases the degree of competition among themselves as they are better adapted to the new environment on average and have lower and tighter distribution of marginal costs. Such convergence in marginal costs makes it easier for a laggard to leapfrog the leader, reducing the overall duration of the industry leadership (or increasing the frequency of leadership changes) and thus raising the intra-industry volatility.

Further evidence on the effect of R&D on the structural volatility is obtained by examining the intensity of firms' R&D in the steady state as observed for different combinations of the two parameters (s and f). There are two measures we look at in this regard. At the industry level, the R&D intensity is captured by the aggregate R&D spending ($\overline{TRD}$). Given the two modes of R&D in the model, innovation and imitation, we also look at $\overline{NRD}$, the share of the innovation cost in the aggregate R&D spending. Figure 6.5 shows the impact of s and f on the two R&D variables.[4]

Property 6.6: Both the aggregate R&D spending and the innovation's share of the R&D expenditure increase with the size of the market and decrease with the size of the fixed cost.

Given the role of endogenous R&D described in Property 6.5, one would expect a higher aggregate R&D spending (in industries with larger market size and smaller fixed cost) to lead to a lower inter-industry volatility and higher intra-industry volatility and vice versa. The results shown in Figure 6.5 are fully consistent with this intuition, when viewed in conjunction with Property 6.3 and Property 6.4.

It is also worthwhile to note that the behavior of the share of the innovation cost in the aggregate R&D spending, as shown in Figure 6.5(b), implies that those industries that exhibit lower inter-industry volatility but higher intra-industry volatility (i.e., those with higher s and lower f) are likely to spend a greater share of R&D expenditure on innovation

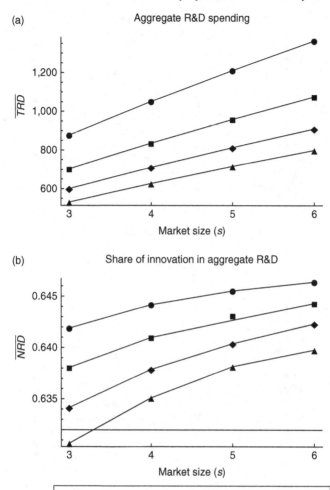

Figure 6.5 Impact of market size (*s*) and fixed cost (*f*) on R&D. (a) Aggregate R&D spending, (b) Share of innovation in aggregate R&D spending

(rather than imitation) than another industry with higher inter-industry volatility but lower intra-industry volatility (i.e., those with lower *s* and higher *f*).

In summary, the negative relationship between the inter-industry volatility and the intra-industry volatility as implied by Property 6.3 and Property 6.4 can be explained on the basis of the differential ways

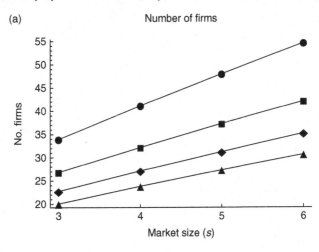

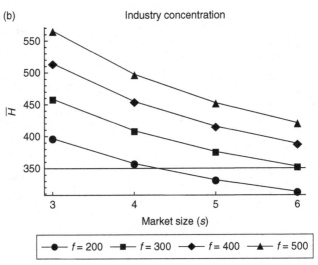

Figure 6.6 Impact of market size (*s*) and fixed cost (*f*) on industry structure. (a) Number of firms, (b) Industry concentration

in which endogenous R&D affect these two measures of structural volatility.

6.3.2 Steady-state structure and performance of an industry

The turnovers described in the previous section have a long-run impact on the steady-state number of firms that an industry can sustain.

Figure 6.6 shows that the number of firms (both active and inactive) increases with *s* and decreases with *f*, while the industry concentration, measured by the Herfindahl-Hirschmann Index, decreases with *s* and increases with *f*. Hence, those industries with a smaller market size and a larger fixed cost are likely to be more concentrated and have a higher rate of turnover.

Property 6.7: The industry concentration decreases with the size of the market and increases with the size of the fixed cost.

It is notable that this result is in line with the predictions of the static equilibrium model of oligopoly, in which the free-entry equilibrium number of firms was directly related to the market size and inversely related to the fixed cost. (See equation (3.10) in Chapter 3.)

Figure 6.7 captures the impacts *s* and *f* have on $\bar{P}$ (market price), $\overline{WMC}$ (industry marginal cost), and $\overline{PCM}$ (industry price-cost margin). All three variables are negatively related to the size of the market and positively related to the fixed cost.

Notice that the market price and the industry price-cost margin are related to the market size and the fixed cost in the same way that the industry concentration is related to the two parameters. They decrease with the market size and increase with the fixed cost. This implies that the price and the price-cost margin are both positively related to market concentration. While this is consistent with the market power explanation behind the concentration-price relationship (or the concentration-price-cost margin relationship), Figure 6.6(a)–(b) and Figure 6.7(b) jointly suggest an alternative explanation. Those industries with smaller market size and larger fixed cost are capable of sustaining a smaller number of firms. The lower degree of competition in a relatively concentrated industry implies a weaker selection pressure on the incumbent firms. Consequently, the steady-state level of the industry marginal cost tends to be higher due to the relative inefficiency of the firms in smaller markets (or the markets with higher fixed cost). This leads to a higher market price. As shown in Figure 6.7(c), the price-cost margin is also higher in those industries with smaller market size and higher fixed cost. These results then suggest that the market power effect and the efficiency effect *jointly* determine the relationship between industry concentration and the market price (or the price-cost margin).

Property 6.8: Both the market price and the industry marginal cost decrease with the size of the market and increase with the size of the fixed cost. The industry price-cost margin also decreases with the size of the market and increases with the size of the fixed cost.

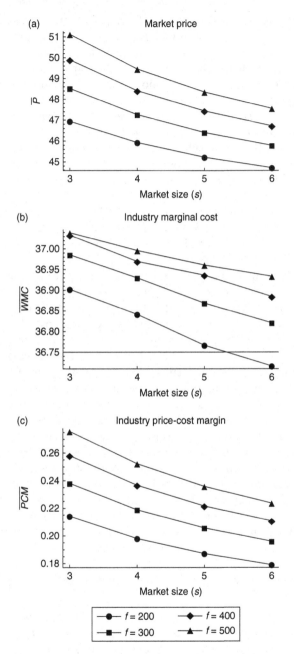

Figure 6.7 Impact of market size (*s*) and fixed cost (*f*) on industry performance. (a) Market price, (b) Industry marginal cost, (c) Industry price-cost margin

It is straightforward to establish the relationships *between* the endogenous variables on the basis of the properties established above. For instance, an industry with a high rate of firm turnover is likely to be highly concentrated. The market price in such an industry is also likely to be high. However, the firms are likely to invest less heavily in R&D, with a relatively greater emphasis on imitation than innovation. The same industry tends to have higher industry marginal cost (and thus be relatively inefficient), but generate higher price-cost margins for the firms. These predicted relationships have implications for cross-sectional empirical research as discussed in the next section.

6.4 Implications for cross-industries studies

Traditional empirical studies in industrial organization, addressing the issues of market structure and performance, are cross-sectional studies of a large number of heterogeneous industries. (See Schmalensee (1989) and Caves (2007) for surveys of this immense literature.) These industries are likely to vary widely in terms of the size of the market they operate in as well as the size of the fixed cost that determines the economies of scale for the firms within each industry. Given the variety of industries, the past empirical studies attempted to identify relationships between variables that are endogenous to the industry dynamics, such as the rate of firm turnover, industry concentration, market price, price-cost margins, and R&D intensities. The comparative dynamics results presented in the previous section can assist us in understanding these cross-sectional relationships within a unifying conceptual framework.

In the context of our model, industries can differ in terms of the two parameters, s and f. Table 6.3 summarizes the relationships between the two parameters and the major endogenous variables as identified in our comparative dynamics exercise in Section 6.3.

There are seven endogenous variables that have the same relationship with respect to the size of the market and the fixed cost: the rate of entry, the rate of exit, industry concentration, duration of industry leadership, market price, industry marginal cost, and industry price-cost margin are all negatively related to s and positively related to f. Conversely, the remaining four variables – the number of firms, the frequency of leadership changes, the aggregate R&D spending, and the cost share of innovation in aggregate R&D – are positively related to s and negatively related to f.

One may infer from Table 6.3 the implicit relationships between the endogenous variables that have been central to many of the cross-sectional studies in industrial organization. First, the number of firms

Table 6.3 Relationships between the industry-specific factors and the endogenous variables

Endogenous variables	Parameters	
	s	f
Rate of entry ($\overline{ER}$)	−	+
Rate of exit ($\overline{XR}$)	−	+
No. firms	+	−
Industry concentration ($\bar{H}$)	−	+
Duration of industry leadership	−	+
Frequency of leadership changes	+	−
Price ($\bar{P}$)	−	+
Industry marginal cost ($\overline{WMC}$)	−	+
Industry price-cost margin ($\overline{PCM}$)	−	+
Aggregate R&D spending ($\overline{TRD}$)	+	−
Share of innovation in aggregate R&D ($\overline{NRD}$)	+	−

and market price are negatively related (or alternatively the industry concentration and market price are positively related). Similarly, the number of firms and the industry price-cost margin are negatively related (i.e., the industry concentration and the industry price-cost margin are positively related).

Property 6.9: Industry concentration is positively related to market price and the industry price-cost margin.

Both of these predictions are consistent with the traditional structure–conduct–performance paradigm that drove much of the cross-sectional studies in the empirical literature. (Weiss (1989) provides a collection of empirical studies that examine these issues in detail. Also see Schmalensee (1989) for a comprehensive survey of the empirical literature in this tradition.)

Second, the rate of entry and the rate of exit are positively related so that an industry with a higher than average rate of entry also has a higher than average rate of exit – i.e., there are high turnover industries and low turnover industries (DRS (1988)). Furthermore, the rate of turnover is positively related to industry concentration so that a concentrated industry tends to have a high *rate* of firm movements in and out of the industry.[5]

Property 6.10: The rate of turnover is positively related to industry concentration.

This also implies that the duration of industry leadership is positively related to industry concentration, while the frequency of leadership changes is negatively related to industry concentration. Hence, market dominance by a single firm is likely to be longer-lasting in a more concentrated industry.

Property 6.11: The duration of industry leadership is positively related to industry concentration.

Third, a high turnover industry tends to have relatively inefficient firms, but the industry price-cost margin tends to be high due to the high market price.

Property 6.12: The rate of turnover is positively related to industry price-cost margin.

Both the R&D intensity as measured by the aggregate R&D spending and the cost share of innovative R&D (rather than imitative R&D) tend to be low in those industries having high turnovers (high inter-industry volatility). Conversely, both R&D variables are high in those industries where the leadership changes are frequent (i.e., high intra-industry volatility).

Property 6.13: The aggregate R&D spending and the cost share of innovative R&D are negatively related to the rate of turnover, but positively related to the frequency of leadership changes.

Notes

1 Their dataset consists of 387 four-digit SIC industries in 1963–1967 and 1967–1972, and 431 four-digit SIC industries in 1972–1977 and 1977–1982 time periods.
2 The Gini coefficient is computed using the market shares of all firms that were in the industry in a given period, t. Hence, it includes all firms in M^t, which is defined after the entry stage but before the exit stage.
3 The cost advantage can emerge for the incumbents even when there is no endogenous R&D, since the selection force of the market competition tends to weed out the relatively inefficient firms from the industry, thereby improving the efficiency of the incumbents on average. The assumption of endogenous R&D further enlarges this relative cost advantage, hence raising the entry barrier, by allowing the incumbents to individually lower their costs as well. This endogenous entry barrier is unlikely to exist when the potential entrants can copy the best available technology of the incumbents at zero cost. But to the extent that the imitation of a technology remains imperfect, the R&D efforts by the incumbents will create a barrier against the potential entrants.
4 It should be noted that the aggregate R&D spending in Property 6.6 is driven by the endogenous number of firms. As will be shown in the next section, the total number of firms that an industry can sustain increases with the market size and decreases with the size of the fixed cost. When the aggregate R&D spending is divided by the number of firms, the resulting R&D spending per firm responds to the changes in the two parameters in exactly the opposite

way: it decreases with the market size and increases with the size of the fixed cost. Since our focus in this section is mainly on the industry-level variables, we stay with the aggregate measure rather than the per-firm measure.

5 It should be noted that this result is specific to the rate of entry or exit. The level (number) of entry or exit is smaller in a more concentrated industry.

7 Firm dynamics in the steady state
Within-industry variations

> [T]he assumption that business behavior is ideally rational and prompt, and also that in principle it is the same with all firms, works tolerably well only within the precincts of tried experience and familiar motive. It breaks down as soon as we leave those precincts and allow the business community under study to be faced by – not simply new situations, which also occur as soon as external factors unexpectedly intrude – but by new possibilities of business action which are as yet untried and about which the most complete command of routine teaches nothing.
> [Schumpeter (1939), p. 98]

Chapter 6 was devoted to studying the aggregate (or average) behavior of firms over time and across industries through the comparative dynamics analysis of the steady states. In this chapter, I go beyond the aggregate behavior and probe deeper into the behavior of individual firms in order to identify any persistent heterogeneity that exists among firms in the same industry. I start by focusing on two types of heterogeneities: 1) technological diversity among firms; and 2) the inequality in market shares held by the competing firms. Variations along these two dimensions are driven by the persistent entries and exits of firms over time as well as the evolving asymmetry in their production efficiencies. This also implies that the firms vary widely in terms of their survivability. The third section of the chapter addresses the variation in firms' life span and the infant mortality phenomenon it implies.

7.1 Technological diversity

7.1.1 R&D reduces technological diversity

To motivate the research questions posed in this chapter, I start with the observation made in Chapter 4 that a typical (baseline) industry in this model displays a *persistent* degree of technological diversity as defined in equation (4.3) – see Figure 4.4(a)–(b). Such persistence in techno-logical diversity is driven by the external shocks to the technological environment. Note that a firm's pursuit of R&D (whether it is innovative or imitative) is adaptive in nature since the R&D activity is modeled as a search process in which all firms try to move closer to the *unique* optimal technology (common to all firms). Given the latest shock to the technological environment, the gradual adaptation (via R&D) by firms reduces the degree of technological diversity within the industry until it is hit by another external shock. When a new technological shock hits, it offers new opportunities for the potential entrants to come in with technologies different from those of the incumbents, temporarily raising the degree of technological diversity in the industry. The mean degree of technological diversity is then the result of the balancing act between the two countervailing forces: 1) the external shocks to the technological environment that raise the degree of diversity through entry of new firms; and 2) the R&D activities of the incumbents that reduce the degree of diversity through improved adaptation to the new technological environment.

In view of the above forces, making firms' R&D endogenous in the model, while holding the rate (γ) and the magnitude (g) of the external shocks fixed, should *decrease* the mean degree of technological diversity ($\overline{DIV}$) along the steady state. I perform a computational experiment based on our model to confirm this intuition. First, for the baseline configuration of the industry parameters, I generate and grow an indus-try with the usual specification that all firms make their R&D decisions endogenously. For the same parameter configuration, I then generate and grow an alternative industry in which firms enter, each endowed with a random technology, but then never perform any R&D (i.e., never adopt any new technology) during their stay in the industry: Hence, the component of the model that allows for endogenous R&D is turned off for this alternative industry.

Under the two specifications I compute the steady-state degree of technological diversity (mean of the diversity measure over the last 2,000 periods between $t = 3,001$ and $t = 5,000$) for each replication. Figure 7.1 shows the histograms of the steady-state means with and without endogenous R&D from 500 independent replications. In line with the intuition provided above, allowing firms to perform R&D reduces the mean degree of technological diversity.

Given the role of endogenous R&D as described above, one could further conjecture that, when R&D is endogenous, the reduction in the cost of R&D (K_{IN} and K_{IM}) will lead to a decline in the steady

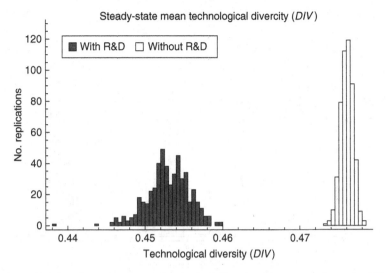

Figure 7.1 Steady-state mean technological diversity: histograms from the 500 independent replications, with and without endogenous R&D

state diversity ($\overline{DIV}$) by inducing firms to raise the aggregate volume of R&D activities. This is verified in a comparative dynamics exercise performed with respect to the fixed costs of R&D (i.e., K_{IN} and K_{IM}), holding all other parameters at their baseline levels.

Figure 7.2 presents the histograms of the steady-state means of the volume of R&D activities as well as those of technological diversity for all 500 replications for four different pairs of K_{IN} and K_{IM}, where K_{IN} is always twice as large as K_{IM}: $(K_{IN}, K_{IM}) \in \{(100,50), (300, 150), (500, 250), (700, 350)\}$.

First, note that the total R&D spending (TRD) is no longer an adequate measure of R&D efforts in this analysis, as it involves varying the costs of R&D themselves: the change in TRD may be due to the change in the volume of R&D activities or that in the costs of R&D. To avoid this problem, we look at the total number of R&D directly (i.e., we count the total number of firms that incurred R&D expense, whether innovative or imitative R&D, at each point in time). Figure 7.2(a) presents the histograms of the steady-state mean number of R&D for the four different cases of (K_{IN}, K_{IM}). As expected, the firms are more active in R&D when the costs of R&D are lower.

Also in line with our intuition, Figure 7.2(b) shows that the distribution of steady-state mean diversity ($\overline{DIV}$) shifts up as the costs of R&D rise. Based on these observations, we conclude:

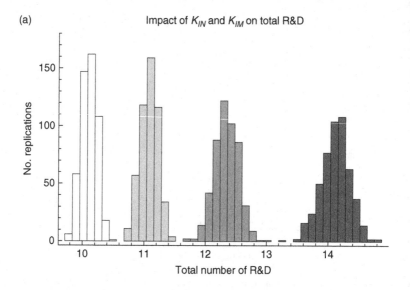

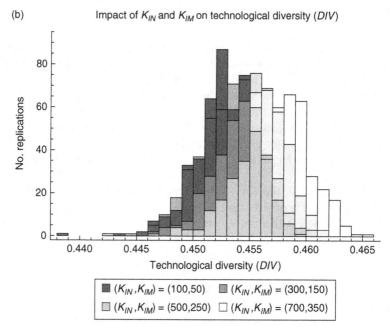

Figure 7.2 Impact of R&D costs, K_{IN} and K_{IM}. (a) Steady-state mean volume of R&D, (b) Steady-state mean technological diversity

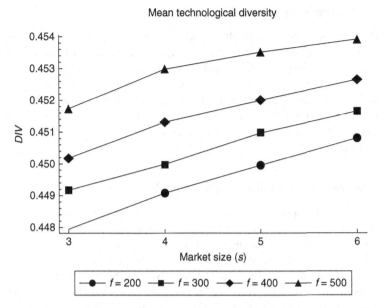

Figure 7.3 Impact of market size (*s*) and fixed cost (*f*) on the steady-state mean technological diversity

Property 7.1: Lower costs of R&D induce higher volume of R&D activities by the firms; consequently, the more intensive search results in reduced technological diversity along the steady state.

7.1.2 Impact of market size and fixed cost on technological diversity

The degree of technological diversity also depends on the values of the two main parameters of the model, *s* and *f*. Figure 7.3 shows that the average value of the steady-state means, $\overline{DIV}$, over 500 replications stays above 0.448 for all parameter values. Furthermore, the following property is identified:

Property 7.2: The mean technological diversity ($\overline{DIV}$) increases with the size of the market (s) and decreases with the size of the fixed cost (f).

Hence, the firms are likely to hold more diverse technologies in larger markets and in those markets with relatively lower fixed cost of production. Since the steady-state number of firms is higher in these markets, the higher degree of technological diversity is driven mainly by the larger population size.

7.2 Market share inequality

The diversity among technologies adopted by firms within a given industry leads to asymmetries in the production efficiencies of these firms. This also implies that there must be significant variation in the market shares held by these firms. The extent of such inequality in any given period may be measured using the Gini coefficient (G^t) as defined in equation (4.4) in Section 4.1. In this section, we examine how endogenous R&D as well as the industry-specific factors such as s and f may affect the steady-state mean inequality, $\bar{G}$.

7.2.1 R&D increases market share inequality

Unequal market shares indicate differences in production efficiencies of the competing firms. Since the long-run efficiency of a firm depends on the extent to which it carries out its R&D activities, a relevant question is how allowing firms to perform R&D affects the steady-state degree of market share inequality. To find an answer to this question, we repeat the computational experiment of the type performed in the previous section, in which two sets of simulations are run, one without endogenous R&D and one with endogenous R&D. Each set of simulations contains 500 independent replications. The steady-state mean of the Gini coefficient, $\bar{G}$, is computed for each of these replications. The histograms of $\bar{G}$ for these 500 replications for the two cases are presented in Figure 7.4. As clearly shown, the market shares are more unequally distributed (i.e., Gini coefficient is higher) when firms are allowed to perform R&D.

Recall from the discussion of "inter-industry volatility" in Section 6.3.1 that the pursuit of R&D allows the incumbent firms to adapt to the changing environment more effectively (relative to potential entrants); hence the reduced inter-industry volatility under endogenous R&D. The general improvement in efficiency of the incumbents, however, increases the degree of competition among themselves, resulting in a lower and tighter distribution of marginal costs for the surviving firms. A slight cost advantage is likely to give the firm a substantial increase in its market share, thus increasing the market share inequality along the steady state.

The above intuition is further supported by the comparative dynamics exercise performed with respect to K_{IN} and K_{IM}. Repeating the procedure from the previous section, we compute the steady-state mean of the Gini coefficient for 500 independent replications for $(K_{IN}, K_{IM}) \in \{(100,50), (300, 150), (500, 250), (700, 350)\}$. In line with our intuition, we observe the following property (see Figure 7.5):

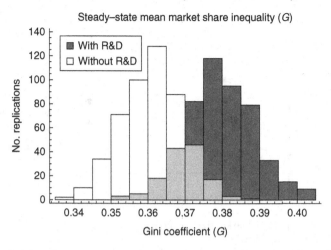

Figure 7.4 Steady-state mean market share inequality: histograms from the 500 independent replications, with and without endogenous R&D

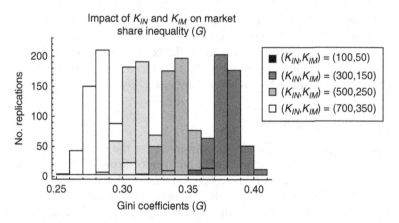

Figure 7.5 Impact of R&D costs, K_{IN} and K_{IM}, on steady-state mean market share inequality

Property 7.3: The market share inequality is higher, when the cost of R&D is lower (and, hence, the volume of R&D is greater).

7.2.2 Impact of market size and fixed cost on market share inequality

Market share inequality also depends on the size of the market (s) and the fixed cost (f). The comparative dynamics results with respect to the two parameters are shown in Figure 7.6.

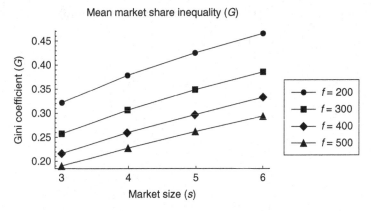

Figure 7.6 Impact of market size (*s*) and fixed cost (*f*) on the steady-state mean market share inequality

Property 7.4: The market share inequality ($\overline{G}$) increases with the size of the market (s) and decreases with the size of the fixed cost (f).

Property 7.2 and Property 7.4 jointly indicate that technological diversity ($\overline{DIV}$) and market share inequality ($\overline{G}$) are positively related when industries are differentiated on the basis of the market size and the fixed cost. Those values of *s* and *f* that lead to high technological diversity also lead to high market share inequality.

7.3 Life span of firms

The persistent entry and exit that characterize the steady state of the industry have an implication for the life span of firms. An industry that has a high rate of turnover should display a relatively shorter life span for an average firm and vice versa. Before engaging in a comparative study of the between-industry variations in this regard, let us first examine the variation in the life span of firms operating within a given industry.

As a point of departure, I suggest that we go back to the entry/exit data from the US automobile industry between 1895 and 1966 (from Chapter 5). The entry and exit data, constructed from Smith (1968), were plotted in Figure 5.2. There were 917 total exits over the period, but there was also wide variation in the ages of the firms at the time of their exit. Some firms exited the same year they entered the market, in which case their life span is zero; others were more fortunate, although, as shown in Figure 5.3, the phenomenon of infant mortality is clearly in display during this time period. The maximum life span was observed to be 62 years.

(a)

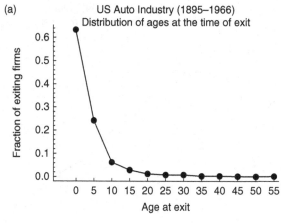

US Auto Industry (1895–1966)
Distribution of ages at the time of exit

(b)

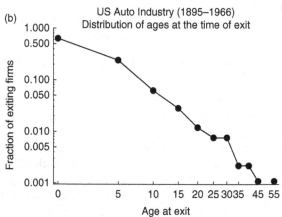

US Auto Industry (1895–1966)
Distribution of ages at the time of exit

Figure 7.7 Distribution of ages of exiting firms in the US auto industry (1895–1966). (a) Linear graph, (b) Log-log graph

Given the data on the ages of firms at the time of their exit, let us produce a histogram of the exit ages by binning them into bins of equal size 5. That is, the first bin goes from 0 to 4, the second from 5 to 9, the third from 10 to 14, and so forth. The resulting histogram is shown in Figure 7.7 (a), where the horizontal axis shows the starting age for each consecutive bin and the vertical axis captures the fraction of all exiting firms which were of ages belonging to each bin. The figure shows that 63 percent of all exiting firms had a life span between 0 and 4, 24 percent had a life span between 5 and 9, 6 percent had a life span between 10 and 14, and so forth.

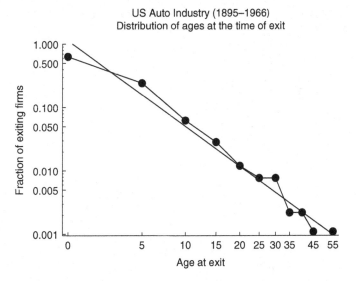

Figure 7.8 Best fit for the distribution of ages of exiting firms in the US auto industry (1895–1966)

Figure 7.7(b) plots the same histogram on a log-log scale. The plot on logarithmic scale is approximately linear, which reveals the power law form of the distribution underlying the life span of firms. To be more specific, let $f(x)dx$ be the fraction of exiting firms with ages between x and $x + dx$. The fact that the histogram is a straight line on log-log scale implies that $\ln f(x) = -\hat{a}\ln x + \hat{c}$, where $\hat{a}$ and $\hat{c}$ are constants. Taking the exponential of both sides, this can be re-written as:

$$f(x) = \hat{C}x^{-\hat{a}}, \qquad (7.1)$$

where $\hat{C} = e^{\hat{c}}$. Distributions that have the above form are said to follow the power law, where the constant $\hat{a}$ is referred to as the *exponent of the power law*.

Given the age-at-exit data from the auto industry, a least-squares fit can be found, where the best fit entails $\hat{a} = 2.83755$ and $\hat{c} = 0.12509$. The fitted line is super-imposed on the actual data in Figure 7.8. The power law distribution appears to characterize the life span of the firms in the US auto industry quite well.

The next question is whether our computational model is capable of predicting this property. To pursue this question, let us randomly pick a replication from the baseline simulations and examine the ages of the

(a)

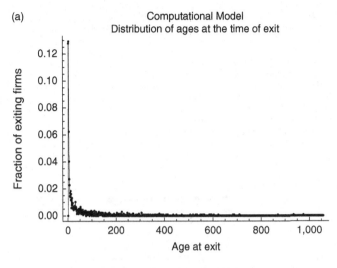

(b)

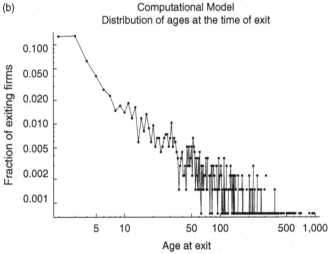

Figure 7.9 Distribution of ages of exiting firms from the computational model (bin size = 1). (a) Linear graph, (b) Log-log graph

exiting firms at the time of each exit that takes place over the steady state between $t = 3,001$ and $t = 5,000$. Figure 7.9(a) shows a histogram of the ages at exit (i.e., life span) for a randomly chosen replication; it had a total of 1,363 exits over the 2,000 periods of steady state. The binning of the ages here is at its most refined such that each bin is of

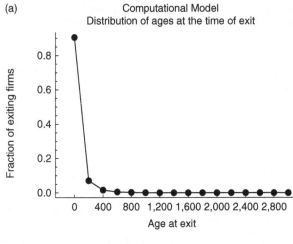

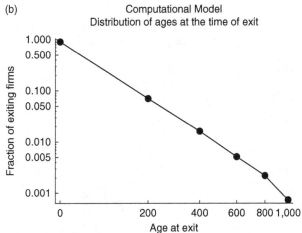

Figure 7.10 Distribution of ages of exiting firms from the computational model (bin size = 200). (a) Linear graph, (b) Log-log graph

size one. There were 174 instances (13 percent) where exiting firms were exactly 1 year old; 176 instances (13 percent) where they were 2 years old; 85 instances (6 percent) where they were 3 years old; 55 instances (4 percent) where they were 4 years old; and so forth. The phenomenon of "infant mortality" is clearly visible in this figure.

More interestingly, when the same histogram is plotted on a log-log scale in Figure 7.9(b), it takes the general shape of a straight line with a negative slope as in the case of the US auto industry. The data toward

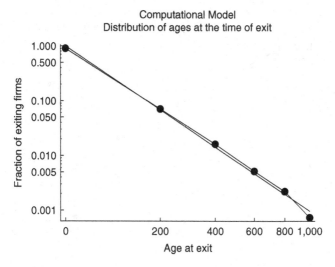

Figure 7.11 Best fit for the distribution of ages of exiting firms from the computational model (bin size = 200)

the tail-end of the distribution are quite noisy, however, and this is due to the bins being of such a small size. To get a smoother plot, we can increase the size of the bin. For instance, suppose we bin the data such that each bin contains exactly 200 age levels: the first bin contains ages 0–199, the second bin contains ages 200–399, and so forth. The resulting histogram is shown in Figure 7.10(a) as a linear plot and 7.10(b) as the log-log plot.

Just as in the case of the US automobile industry, the model predicts the life span of firms to be characterized by power law distribution. The best fit for the data captured in Figure 7.10 entails $\hat{a} = 3.87739$ and $\hat{c} = 0.003927$. The fitted line is plotted with the model-generated data in Figure 7.11. The fit is almost perfect.

In line with the previous analyses on diversity and inequality, I now consider the impact endogenous R&D has on the distribution of firms' ages at the time of exit. I collect the age-at-exit data from the 500 independent replications performed under two separate specifications, one where R&D is made endogenous and one where R&D is completely turned off.

The collected data from a random replication under the two specifications are plotted together on a log-log scale in Figure 7.12. Notice that it indicates the distribution of age-at-exit (life span) as being lower when firms do not perform any R&D. A careful examination of the data for

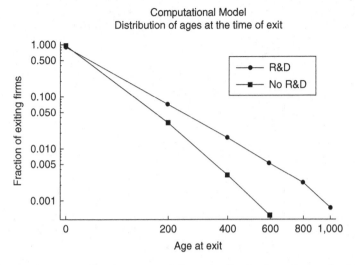

Figure 7.12 Impact of endogenous R&D on the distribution of ages of exiting firms from the computational model (bin size = 200)

Table 7.1 Fitted value of the exponent for the power law ($\hat{a}$)

$\ln f(x) = -\hat{a} \ln x - \hat{c}$

	f = 200	f = 300	f = 400	f = 500
s = 3	4.02977	4.29375	4.44048	4.51863
	(0.305441)	(0.353486)	(0.384022)	(0.423841)
s = 4	3.76913	4.04658	4.21939	4.34876
	(0.295897)	(0.323955)	(0.362293)	(0.376611)
s = 5	3.56886	3.85695	4.09201	4.20512
	(0.234936)	(0.304432)	(0.322524)	(0.361473)
s = 6	3.40564	3.71631	3.90947	4.06501
	(0.215558)	(0.270477)	(0.289772)	(0.328204)

all 500 replications under each specification confirms that this is a general property. In fact, the mean exponent of the power law (i.e., averaged over 500 replications) is $\hat{a}$ = 3.76913 (0.295897) with R&D and is $\hat{a}$ = 5.23248 (0.349334) without R&D. (The number inside the parenthesis is the standard deviation.) Hence, *endogenous R&D increases the life span of a firm*.

We can also see the impact of the two parameters, f and s, on the exponent of the power law ($\hat{a}$). Table 7.1 reports the exponent, averaged

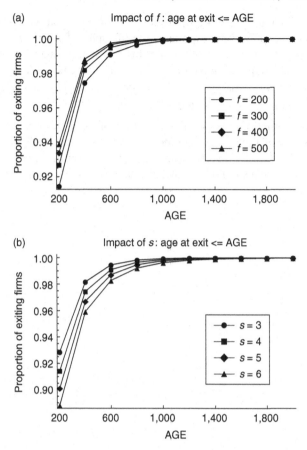

Figure 7.13 Proportion of firms exiting the industry that were of a given age (AGE) or younger. (a) Impact of fixed cost (*f*), (b) Impact of market size (*s*)

over 500 replications, for each parameter configuration. We observe that the exponent decreases with the size of the market (*s*) and increases with the size of the fixed cost (*f*).

To get a more intuitive perspective on how the two parameters, *f* and *s*, affect the life span of firms, I further derive the *cumulative density* of a given age-at-exit by asking what proportion of all exiting firms exited at a given age (AGE) or younger – this is the same type of information that was displayed in Figure 5.3 for the US auto industry. This information is plotted in Figure 7.13(a) for $f \in \{200, 300, 400, 500\}$ given $s = 4$; and

Figure 7.13(b) for $s \in \{3,4,5,6\}$ given $f=200$. Consistent with the observation on the power law exponent, the life span of a firm tends to be shorter (i.e., a larger proportion of firms exit at a given age or younger) when the fixed cost is higher and/or the market size is smaller.

Property 7.5: The average life span of a firm decreases with the size of the market (s) and increases with the size of the fixed cost (f).

Recall from Property 6.3 that the rate of firm turnover decreases with the size of the market and increases with the size of the fixed cost. Property 7.5 follows directly from that observation in that the average life span of a firm should be shorter in those industries with higher rates of firm turnover.

8 Cyclical industrial dynamics with fluctuating demand

> Business cycles are not merely fluctuations in aggregate economic activity. The critical feature that distinguishes them from the commercial convulsions of earlier centuries or from the seasonal and other short term variations of our own age is that the fluctuations are widely diffused over the economy – its industry, its commercial dealings, and its tangles of finance. The economy of the western world is a system of closely interrelated parts. He who would understand business cycles must master the workings of an economic system organized largely in a network of free enterprises searching for profit. The problem of how business cycles come about is therefore inseparable from the problem of how a capitalist economy functions.
>
> [Burns (1951), p. 3]

The fluctuations of many industries often correlate with those in the aggregate economy (business cycle), though to a varying degree of sensitivity. For example, a large body of empirical literature in the areas of macroeconomics and industrial organization has made the following observations:

1. *Firm entry and business formation are procyclical.*
2. *The price level and the average mark-ups by firms are countercyclical.*
3. *The R&D activities are procyclical.*

Chatterjee et al., (1993) consider stationary sunspot equilibrium and endogenous cycles in a two-sector overlapping-generations model with entry. The equilibrium they derive offers several empirical implications: 1) Net business formation is procyclical; 2) mark-ups are countercyclical; and 3) prices are countercyclical. In a business cycle model of monopolistic competition, Devereux et al., (1996) generate entry and exit of firms over the cycle through technology shocks. Their model predicts procyclical net entry of firms and, hence, the number of firms increases in the event of a positive technology shock (a boom). The empirical evidence on the procyclical net business formation and countercyclical mark-ups is also provided in Etro and Colciago (2010).

Many researchers have found, both empirically and theoretically, that mark-ups are countercyclical and negatively correlated with the number of competitors (Bils (1987), Chatterjee et al., (1993), Rotemberg and Woodford (1990, 1999), Warner and Barsky (1995), Chevalier and Scharfstein (1996), MacDonald (2000), Chevalier et al., (2003)). Martins, Scapetta, and Pilat (1996) cover different industries in 14 OECD countries and find mark-ups to be countercyclical in 53 of the 56 cases they consider, with statistically significant results in most of these. In addition, these authors conclude that entry rates have a negative and statistically significant correlation with mark-ups. Bresnahan and Reiss (1991) find that an increase in the number of producers increases the competitiveness in the markets they analyze. Campbell and Hopenhayn (2005) provide empirical evidence to support the argument that firms' pricing decisions are affected by the number of competitors they face; they show that mark-ups react negatively to increases in the number of firms.

Rotemberg and Saloner (1986) provide empirical evidence of countercyclical price movements and offer a model of collusive pricing when demand is subject to i.i.d. shocks. Their model generates countercyclical collusion and predicts countercyclical pricing. (Haltiwanger and Harrington (1991) and Kandori (1991) offer models that provide further support for the theory, though Green and Porter (1984) develop a model of trigger pricing which predicts positive co-movement of prices and demand.) Etro and Colciago (2010) examines the endogenous market structure under Bertrand and Cournot competition in a DSGE (Dynamic Stochastic General Equilibrium) model and find: 1) entry of new firms is procyclical; 2) individual and aggregate profits are procyclical; and 3) mark-ups are countercyclical.

Comin and Gertler (2006) present evidence on medium-term business cycles and show that R&D tends to move procyclically. The real business cycle model they develop allows for R&D, technology adoption, and variation in mark-ups and is capable of making predictions that are consistent with the empirical findings. Barlevy (2007) shows the procyclicality of R&D, using both the NSF data and the Compustat data. He then constructs a real business cycle model that includes an innovation sector, in which production and R&D compete for labor resources. The cyclical behavior of R&D is then driven by the fluctuations over time in the relative productivity of the two uses.

In this chapter, I contribute to this voluminous literature by exploring these empirical regularities using the computational model of industry dynamics. I show that our model is capable of replicating all of the above-mentioned regularities and, more importantly, identifying the underlying mechanism that gives rise to these regularities within a single coherent framework.

8.1 An overview

One way in which fluctuations at the industry-level are connected to those at the economy-level is through the movement in the size of the market demand that results from the economy-wide fluctuations. This chapter focuses on how fluctuations in market demand, whatever their cause, affect the evolutionary dynamics of the industry and ultimately induce cyclical patterns in certain endogenous variables.

As shown in the previous chapters, the proposed model is capable of generating *persistent* entries and exits of firms based solely on the shocks to technological environment. In this chapter, we add fluctuations in market demand to the baseline model in order to identify the relationship between the demand movement and the adaptive behavior of firms over time. This entails systematically varying the size of the market demand, s, while allowing the firms to respond to these changes by adjusting their entry and exit decisions as well as their R&D investment and production decisions.

With the addition of demand fluctuation, the external shocks can come in two different forms: 1) supply shock through the change in the technological environment and 2) demand shock through the change in the size of market demand. Theoretically, there is no *a priori* reason why one type of shock should occur at a higher or lower rate than another. However, in order to focus on the impact of demand-side fluctuations, I apply shocks to the market size (s) at a much lower rate than the shocks to the technological environment. Hence, the firms' adaptive behavior toward fluctuating demand internalizes their response to the more frequent technological shocks.

I first consider a serially correlated stochastic movement in market size (s) with a parameter that captures the rate of *persistence* in demand. With this specification, I show that the model is capable of predicting *cyclical* industry dynamics consistent with the empirical observations. In order to identify the causal and contributing factors of such cyclical patterns, I then consider a deterministic demand cycle, in which the market size variable follows a *sine* wave. This specification, though restrictive, permits a clear look at the underlying process, in which firms systematically adapt to the changing market conditions, endogenously generating the cyclical patterns in the way the industry evolves.

For both specifications the computational exercise entails the usual series of simulation runs, each of which starts out with an empty industry targeted by a fixed-sized pool of potential entrants (refreshed each period). Each run generates the time series data on various endogenous variables that characterize the behavior of firms over the horizon of 5,000 periods. I follow the movements of firms in and out of the market as well as those of other endogenous variables.

Central to our analysis is the identification and characterization of cyclicality in the movements of market price (P^t), industry marginal cost (WMC^t), price-cost margin (PCM^t), aggregate profits (Π^t), and the aggregate R&D expenditure $\left(\sum_{\forall i \in M^t} I_i^t \right)$. The simulation results indicate that the cyclicality in price and price-cost margin are crucially related to the cyclicality in entry/exit dynamics as well as in R&D spending by the firms. First, both entry and exit are procyclical, but entry dominates during the boom, while exit dominates during the bust. This leads to the number of firms rising during a boom and declining during a bust; hence, the countercyclical industry concentration. This change in the industry structure has a significant implication for the degree of competition in the market. The increased number of firms during a boom raises the degree of competition, while the decrease in the number of firms during a bust reduces the degree of competition. The result is that the market price moves "countercyclically" while the industry output and the aggregate revenue move "procyclically."

The industry average marginal cost (WMC^t) also displays countercyclicality, i.e., the average productivity of the firms is procyclical. There are two sources for this. First, the increased competition during a boom potentially raises the selection pressure on the firms, driving out the inefficient firms to a greater extent, hence reducing the marginal costs of surviving firms on average. The reduced degree of competition during a bust will have exactly the opposite effect. This "selection effect" can induce the average marginal cost for the industry to move countercyclically. Second, any cyclical tendency in the endogenous R&D activities of the firms may induce cyclicality in the firms' marginal costs – i.e., "adaptation effect." While both effects are present in our model, the results obtained in this chapter show that the countercyclicality in the average marginal cost is due more to the "adaptation effect" from the endogenous R&D than the "selection effect." In fact, the model predicts the aggregate R&D spending to be procyclical such that there are more intense R&D activities during a boom than during a bust. Given that the role of R&D in this model is to reduce the marginal cost of production, the procyclical aggregate R&D induces countercyclical average marginal cost through the adaptation effect.

Although both the market price and the industry average marginal cost are countercyclical, the variation in price tends to exceed that in the average marginal cost so that the price/marginal cost mark-ups or the price-cost margins are countercyclical. As discussed earlier, there is a large body of applied and theoretical works in macroeconomics and industrial organization that show countercyclical price and mark-ups at the aggregate economy-level or at the industry-level. The media coverage of the oligopoly pricing behavior during the severe economic downturn of 2008–2009 provides further support for these findings:

> Shoppers continue to pare back spending even on basic household staples, resulting in lower-than-expected sales for Procter & Gamble Co. and Colgate-Palmolive Co. The consumer-products giants are responding by raising prices to keep profits from plunging. ... To offset higher commodity prices and global currency swings, P&G and Colgate raised prices in the quarter through March. P&G said higher prices increased its total sales by 7%. Colgate raised prices by 8%.
>
> [Byron (2009), p. B1]

> The nation's two largest brewers by sales are planning a new round of price increases this fall despite flat volumes, in a sign of their growing clout. Anheuser-Busch InBev NV, the largest US beer seller by revenue, and MillerCoors LLC will increase beer prices in the majority of their US sales regions, the two companies said Tuesday. "We do plan on taking prices up in the fall on the majority of our volume in the majority of the US," said David Peacock, president of Anheuser's US division. "The environment is very favorable, we think." ... MillerCoors also said it will raise prices. "We have seen very strong pricing to date this year, and we are projecting a favorable pricing environment moving forward," said Brad Schwartz, a vice president at MillerCoors ... Both US giants have reported strong profits this year, in part by raising prices to offset flat volumes.
>
> [Kesmodel (2009), p. B1]

This chapter provides an explanation for such cyclical pricing behavior within a framework based on the process of firm entry and exit as well as the Schumpeterian process of creative destruction driven by endogenous R&D.

8.2 Stochastic variation in demand

Consider the following stochastic variation in market size:

$$s^t = \begin{cases} \hat{s} & for\ 1 \leq t \leq 2,000; \\ max\{0.1,(1-\theta)\hat{s}+\theta s^{t-1}+\varepsilon^t\} & for\ t \geq 2,001 \end{cases} \tag{8.1}$$

where $\hat{s}$ is the pre-specified mean of the market size (taking the value of 4 in our simulations), θ is the rate of persistence in demand, and ε^t is the random noise. ε^t is assumed to be uniformly distributed between $-1/2$ and $1/2$.

The size of the market, $\hat{s}$, is held fixed at 4 for the first 2,000 periods in order to give the industry sufficient time to attain its structural stability, i.e., the total number of firms achieves a steady state in which it fluctuates around a steady mean. Starting at $t = 2,001$, the market size follows the adjustment dynamic specified above (with the lower bound of 0.1). After allowing another 1,000 periods for the industry to adjust to the cyclical movement in demand, we analyze the time series data from the last 2,000 periods between $t = 3,001$ and $t = 5,000$.

Note that a higher value for θ implies a demand which is more sticky. An important issue is how the persistence (stickiness) in demand affects the cyclicality of various endogenous variables. For the simulations reported here, six different values were considered for θ: $\theta \in \{0.5, 0.7, 0.9, 0.925, 0.95, 0.97\}$. All other parameters were held at the baseline levels as indicated in Table 4.1. For each value of θ, 500 independent replications were performed as usual, each with a fresh set of random numbers.

Figure 8.1 plots the typical movements of the four main endogenous variables – total number of firms, price, industry profits, and the aggregate R&D spending – against the movement of the market size variable, s^t, over a randomly chosen interval of 100 consecutive periods from a single randomly chosen replication. The dotted curve is the movement of s^t, while the solid curve is the movement of the given endogenous variable. The persistence parameter, θ, is set at 0.95 for this particular run.[1] A casual look at these time series tells us that the number of firms is procyclical, the market price is countercyclical, the industry profit is

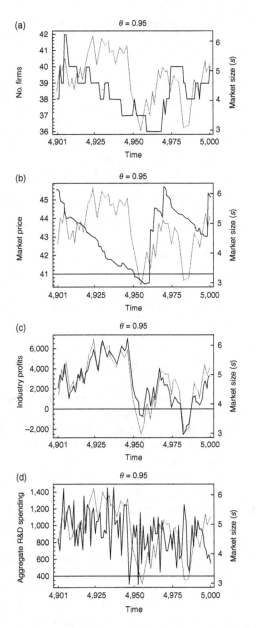

Figure 8.1 Industry dynamics when market size is stochastic. (a) Number of firms, (b) Market price, (c) Industry profits, (d) Aggregate R&D spending

Table 8.1 Correlations between the market size and the endogenous variables

Endogenous variables	θ					
	0.5	0.7	0.9	0.925	0.95	0.97
No. entrants	0.09385	0.10322	0.11657	0.13325	0.14074	0.14148
No. exits	−0.02651	−0.02146	0.00302	0.01844	0.03402	0.03905
Net entrants	0.10772	0.11217	0.10308	0.10483	0.09881	0.09600
No. op. firms	0.04851	0.07692	0.21689	0.28875	0.38755	0.49843
HHI	−0.05983	−0.11142	−0.28404	−0.36813	−0.47827	−0.59718
Price	−0.02475	−0.04946	−0.15846	−0.19263	−0.27268	−0.40277
Ind. marg. cost	0.00124	−0.00054	−0.02488	−0.01479	−0.02655	−0.08369
Industry output	0.99753	0.99831	0.99935	0.99950	0.99966	0.99977
Industry revenue	0.95174	0.96588	0.98592	0.98917	0.99263	0.99487
Industry profit	0.38035	0.41818	0.52905	0.54896	0.58590	0.61795
Price-cost margin	−0.03963	−0.07303	−0.18285	−0.25287	−0.34080	−0.44020
Aggregate R&D	0.01635	0.03713	0.11378	0.15973	0.22659	0.31631

strongly procyclical, and the aggregate R&D spending is moderately procyclical.

To see if these cyclical tendencies are inherent to the system and not just limited to the single run, I examine the correlation between the time series on the realized market demand (s^t) and the time series output of the endogenous variable between $t = 3,001$ and $t = 5,000$. For each endogenous variable, such correlation coefficient was calculated for each replication. Table 8.1 reports the average of those correlations from 500 independent replications for each variable. First, note that the number of entrants is positively correlated with the market size, while the number of exits is weakly or not at all correlated. As the result, the net entrants are positively correlated with the market size. This leads to the number of firms being *positively* correlated with the market size. Hence, the number of firms shows a procyclical tendency, while the degree of industry concentration, H^t, shows a countercyclical tendency.

As glimpsed from the time series in Figure 8.1(b), the market price is countercyclical – i.e., it is *negatively* correlated with the market size. Industry marginal cost is *negatively* correlated with the market size, though the correlation is rather weak. The aggregate R&D spending is procyclical. Both the aggregate output and the aggregate revenue are almost perfectly correlated with the market size. The industry profit is also strongly positively correlated. On the other hand, the industry price-cost margin is negatively correlated with the market size, showing a countercyclical tendency.

All of the results are consistent with the stylized facts reported in the empirical literature. Furthermore, the degree of demand persistence, θ, appears to affect the cyclicality of these variables in a systematic manner. Comparing the correlations between the different values of θ, an increase in θ generally strengthens the cyclicality – i.e., with the exceptions of the number of exits and net entrants, the correlations (positive or negative) are uniformly stronger for a higher value of θ.

8.3 Deterministic variation in demand

To delve into the underlying causal factors of the cyclical patterns, I now consider a deterministic path for s^t as defined by a sine wave:

$$
s^t = \begin{cases} \hat{s} & for\, 1 \le t \le 2,000; \\ \hat{s} + \sigma \sin\left[\dfrac{\pi}{\tau} - t\right] & for\, t \ge 2,001; \end{cases} \tag{8.2}
$$

where $\hat{s}$ (=4) is the pre-specified mean market size, σ is the amplitude of the wave, and τ is the period for half-turn (hence, one period is 2τ). π in the equation is the usual mathematical constant which is approximately equal to 3.14159.

For simulations reported in this book, $\sigma = 2$ and $\tau = 500$. As before, the size of the market is held fixed at 4 for the first 2,000 periods in order to give the industry sufficient time to attain its structural stability. Our analysis focuses on the last 2,000 periods from $t = 3,001$ to $t = 5,000$. Figure 8.2 captures the demand cycle over the relevant period, given the specified parameter values. As noted before, the reported value of an endogenous variable at each point in the time series is the average of the corresponding values from the 500 independent replications.

We first examine the movement of the market price, given the cyclical movement of the market size. Figure 8.3(a) shows the price path (solid curve), along with the deterministic path taken by the market size, s^t (dashed curve).

Property 8.1: Market price is countercyclical.

While the price is countercyclical, the industry profit is approximately, though not perfectly, procyclical – see Figure 8.3(b): The aggregate profits cycle tends to precede the demand cycle such that it peaks when the market size is still rising.

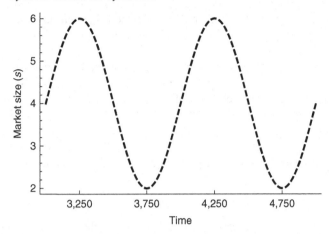

Figure 8.2 Deterministic demand cycle

Property 8.2: Industry aggregate profits are procyclical.

In order to understand these properties, we explore the impact of demand cycle on the movement of firms and the evolving structure of the industry. Figures 8.4(a) and 8.4(b) show the number of entries and the number of exits over time. A rise (fall) in market demand generally increases (decreases) the number of entrants, though the two movements are not perfectly correlated. When the demand is increasing, the number of entrants tends to rise as long as the demand rises at an increasing rate. When the demand rises at a diminishing rate, the number of entrants tends to fall. Likewise, along the downward segment of the demand cycle, the number of entrants falls as long as the demand falls at an increasing rate; once the fall in demand slows down, firms start to enter in rising numbers. Together, these properties imply that the entry cycle tends to precede the demand cycle.

The number of exits follows similar cyclical pattern as the number of entries – see Figure 8.4(b). This indicates *co-movement* of entry and exit over time such that the period with a relatively high number of entrants also has a relatively high number of exits. That is, the industry during a boom is characterized by a greater degree of *turbulence* (i.e., inter-industry volatility) than during a bust. However, the net entry (i.e., the number of entrants minus the number of exits) exhibits procyclicality such that the total number of firms in a given period tends to be procyclical as well – see Figure 8.4(c). Naturally, the time series on the Herfindahl-Hirschmann Index (measuring the concentration of the industry) follows a countercyclical path, as shown in Figure 8.4(d).

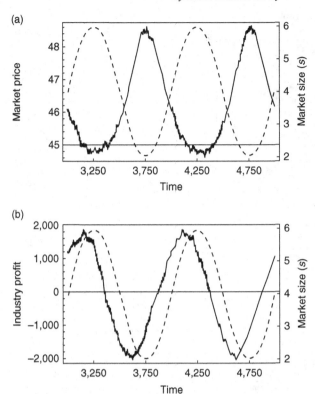

Figure 8.3 Cyclical dynamics of market price and industry profits. (a) Market price, (b) Industry profits

Property 8.3: The number of firms is procyclical (and the industry concentration is countercyclical).

An implication of this property is that the degree of competition is higher during a boom than during a bust. This offers a market power-based explanation as to why we observe countercyclicality in the market price in Property 8.1: The *higher* number of entrants during a boom increases the degree of competition and pushes the price down, while the *lower* number of entrants during a bust reduces the degree of competition and pushes the price up.

Figure 8.5(a) shows that the average price-cost margin is countercyclical.

Property 8.4: The industry average price-cost margin is countercyclical.

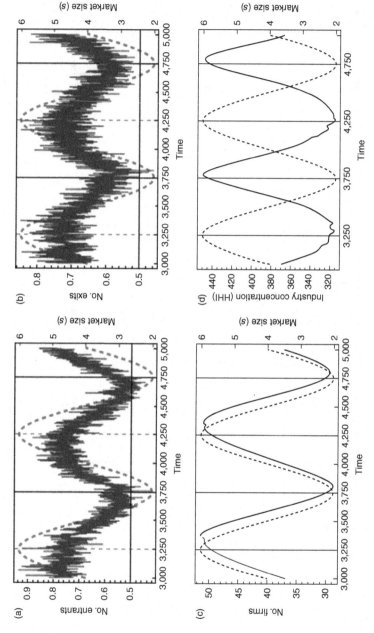

Figure 8.4 Cyclical dynamics of industry structure. (a) Number of entrants, (b) Number of exits, (c) Number of firms, (d) Industry concentration (HHI)

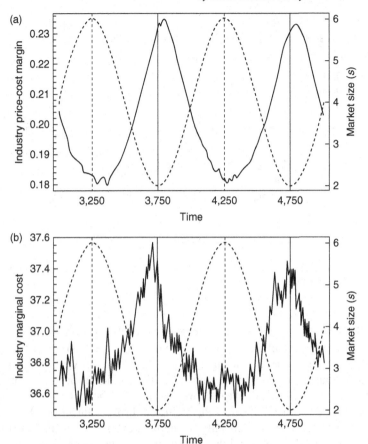

Figure 8.5 Cyclical dynamics of industry performance. (a) Industry price-cost margin, (b) Industry marginal cost

This property can be explained solely on the basis of the countercyclical price, if the marginal costs of the firms remain constant over time. However, that is not the case. The industry marginal cost tends to fluctuate over time as the degree of competition fluctuates. Its movement is induced by: 1) the cyclical firm entries and exits; and 2) the movements in the R&D activities of the surviving firms. Indeed, Figure 8.5(b) shows that the industry marginal cost, WMC^t, is countercyclical: Firms are more efficient during a boom than during a bust.

Property 8.5: The industry average marginal cost is countercyclical.

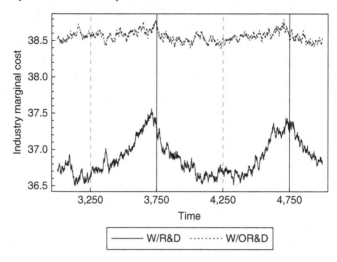

Figure 8.6 Cyclical dynamics of industry marginal cost with and without endogenous R&D

This result would seem consistent with our observation on the entry/exit dynamics, which showed that the market is more (less) competitive – hence, more selective – during a boom (than a bust): A more selective market during a boom should push out the inefficient firms and bring the average marginal cost to a lower level, while the less selective market during the bust may allow the inefficient firms to linger on. A closer look at the source of cyclicality in the firm efficiency reveals that this explanation, though certainly correct, is secondary to another causal factor.

For a more systematic analysis I performed two separate simulations, where the R&D decisions were turned on for one while they were turned off for another. Figure 8.6 reports the industry average marginal costs (WMC^t) over the period of 3,001–5,000, given the demand cycle (with the dashed vertical line representing the period of peak and the solid vertical line representing the trough). The upper series is from the simulation *without* the R&D and the lower series is from the one *with* the R&D. The average marginal cost is only weakly countercyclical when there is no R&D. In contrast, the time series from the model with the endogenous R&D show strong countercyclicality. It is then clear that the cyclical pattern in the industry average marginal cost is driven largely by the cyclicality of endogenous R&D; the changing intensity of market selection from entry and exit has a relatively small impact

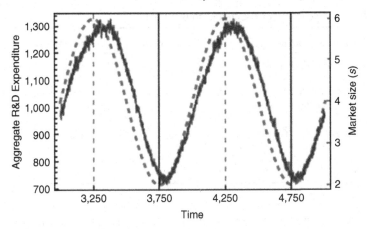

Figure 8.7 Cyclical dynamics of aggregate R&D spending

on the efficiencies of the firms in the industry. The time series on the aggregate R&D spending captured in Figure 8.7 reinforces this interpretation: The aggregate R&D spending by firms displays a procyclical pattern such that the R&D activities are more intense during a boom than during a bust, which contributes to the countercyclicality in the industry marginal cost.

Property 8.6: The aggregate R&D is procyclical.

That firms tend to be more efficient during a boom than a bust (i.e., countercyclical marginal costs) then has an adaptation-based explanation rather than a selection-based explanation. This cyclical tendency is likely to be weaker in those industries in which R&D spending makes up a smaller portion of its total production cost.

Note that the countercyclicality in the average price-cost margin is not obvious, given countercyclicality in both price (Property 8.1) and the average marginal cost (Property 8.5). What is clear is that the firms raise their mark-ups over marginal cost during a bust and reduce them during a boom, which implies that the inter-temporal variation in price is greater than that in the industry marginal cost.

8.4 Summary

Given the underlying framework for the industrial dynamics, the focus of this chapter was on investigating how fluctuations in market demand

Table 8.2 Cyclicality of the endogenous variables

Endogenous variables	Procyclical	Countercyclical
Number of entries ($|E^t|$)	√	
Number of exits ($|L^t_i|$)	√	
No. operating firms ($|M^t|$)	√	
Industry concentration (H^t)		√
Price (P^t)		√
Industry profits (Π^t)	√	
Industry marginal cost (WMC^t)		√
Industry price-cost margin (PCM^t)		√
Aggregate R&D spending (TRD^t)	√	

affect the long-run dynamics of the industry. Two specifications were considered for the inter-temporal movement of market demand. The first was a serially correlated stochastic movement with a parameter that captures the rate of persistence in demand. The second, used for the purpose of identifying the causal factors, was a deterministic cycle, in which the market size variable followed a sine wave, thereby capturing the regular boom-bust cycle with a fixed frequency.

The simulation results, summarized in Table 8.2, are consistent with the cyclical patterns observed empirically for many of the relevant variables. In particular, the entry/exit dynamics that responded to the fluctuation in market demand generated countercyclical industry concentration. The cyclical concentration had implications for fluctuations in the market power of the firms, which in turn led to countercyclical market price. The aggregate R&D spending was shown to be procyclical, generating countercyclical industry marginal costs (and countercyclical price). The mark-ups over marginal costs were greater during a bust than during a boom, which gave rise to the countercyclical price-cost margins. Finally, the more persistent the market demand, the stronger was the degree of cyclicality in these endogenous variables.

Note

1 Note that $\theta = 0.95$ implies the market size may change every 20 periods on average. In contrast, the baseline rate of the technology shock, $\gamma = 0.1$, implies that the technological environment can change every 10 periods on average. Hence, the rate of change in technological environment is twice as high as the rate of change in market demand.

9 Conclusion

> Much of economic analysis is concerned with predicting, explaining, evaluating, or prescribing change. Presumably, then, the adequacy of a theory of firm and industry behavior should be assessed in good part in terms of the light it sheds on such phenomena as the response of firms and the industry as a whole to exogenous change in market conditions, or how it illuminates the sources and consequences of innovation. ... [O]rthodox theory tends to deal in an ad hoc way with the first problem, and ignores or deals mechanically with the second.
>
> [Nelson and Winter (1982), p. 24]

The Schumpeterian process of *creative destruction* is often conceptualized as the Darwinian evolutionary process. The model of industry dynamics proposed here can be viewed in a similar framework. It has two interacting mechanisms that jointly determine how a given industry will evolve over time. The first is the mechanism that generates and maintains technological variation in the population of firms (and, hence, the varying degrees of production efficiency on the supply-side). What guarantees the generation and maintenance of such variation is the inherent tendency of the firms to pursue available profit opportunities, not only in their choices of output, but in the persistent entry by new firms and the R&D efforts of the existing firms. Additionally, the exogenous shocks to the technological environment provide a continuous incentive for firm R&D even in the long run. The second mechanism, interacting with the first, is the market competition of sufficient severity that induces the survival of only a subset of firms from the existing population, where the survival advantage goes to those firms with the technologies giving the lowest cost in the current environment. It is the continuing interaction of these two mechanisms that drive the process of industrial dynamics in the model presented here.

The evolutionary process of Schumpeterian competition was implemented in this study using an agent-based computational model, in which artificial industries were created and grown to maturity *in silico*. While the firms in the model were assumed to have bounded rationality, they were nevertheless adaptive in the sense that their experience-based R&D efforts allowed them to search for improved technologies. In the early phase the means and variances of industry data change, but the external shocks that perennially occur never allow the industry to achieve a truly "static" equilibrium. Given a technological environment subject to persistent and unexpected external shocks, the computationally generated industry remains in a perennial state of flux. More precisely, once past the transient growth phase, it reaches a *steady state* in which the measured behavior of the firms and the industry stochastically fluctuate around steady means. The main objective of the study was to identify the patterns that exist in the *movements* of the firms as the industry evolves over time along the steady state. The detailed investigation of the non-equilibrium adjustment dynamics by firms, as carried out here, is not feasible with the standard equilibrium IO models.

The ultimate value of any model, of course, depends on its capacity to make predictions that can match data. I started the book with four stylized facts from the empirical IO literature: 1) shakeouts in infant industries; 2) persistent entries and exits in mature industries; 3) positive correlation between the entry and the exit time series of a typical industry; and 4) positive correlation between entry and exit across different industries. The computational model developed in this book was able to replicate all of these phenomena, both along the transient growth phase and the steady state phase of the industry. Furthermore, I was able to identify other patterns inherent in the steady-state dynamics of a given industry, as well as variations in those patterns across industries with different characteristics, by systematically varying the characteristics of the market and the technological environment within which the computationally generated industry evolves. This was implemented by performing comparative dynamics analyses on various endogenous variables with respect to the two main parameters of the model, the size of the market (s) and the fixed cost (f). The following results were generated from these analyses, many of which are consistent with the existing empirical literature.

First, in the realm of results that could fall under the rubric of comparative statics, those industries with a higher market size and/or lower fixed cost, call them HSLF industries, were shown to have a larger carrying capacity such that the endogenous number of firms in the steady state is larger; hence these industries are less concentrated than those with a smaller market size and/or a higher fixed cost. Second, the HSLF industries exhibit lower market price and lower price-cost margins along the steady state, thus predicting a positive relationship between concentration and price (or price-cost margins).

More significantly, our model produced results on the *dynamics* of firms and the industry. The HSLF industries are *externally* less turbulent in that they have a lower rate of turnover. However, these industries are also *internally* more turbulent in that they have more frequent changes in the market leadership. The distinct ways in which the two industry-specific factors affect the inter- and intra-industry volatilities can be explained through the R&D activities of firms. The firms in HSLF industries spend more on R&D on aggregate (and also invest more on *innovative* R&D than *imitative* R&D) along the steady state. The more intensive R&D efforts endogenously create an entry barrier by improving the average efficiency of the incumbents relative to that of the potential entrants. This endogenous entry barrier reduces the inter-industry volatility, protecting the incumbents from potential competition. The other side of the same coin, however, is that the more intensive R&D, which is adaptive in nature, also leads to more intense competition among incumbents by reducing their technological diversity. The consequent narrowing of the efficiency differentials results in higher intra-industry volatility.

Given the persistent technological diversity and the perpetual entry and exit of firms over time, there are substantial variations in the efficiency of firms within an industry at any given point in time. These variations, in turn, have implications for the survivability of technologically heterogeneous firms. In the third set of results, consistent with the empirical observations, our model predicts a wide variation in the life span of firms, distribution of which can be characterized by the power law distribution. Furthermore, a close look at the ages of the exiting firms indicates a clear case of infant mortality phenomenon, and the comparative dynamics analysis predicts the average life span of a firm to be longer in those industries with a larger market size and/or a lower fixed cost (HSLF). The latter result is consistent with the earlier result that the inter-industry volatility is lower in the HSLF industries.

Finally, the model and the analysis were extended to investigate the effect of fluctuating demand on industry dynamics. When the size of the market was allowed to fluctuate, the time series of the relevant endogenous variables displayed cyclical patterns that matched four empirical findings from the macroeconomic and IO literature: 1) firm entries and the total number of firms were found to be procyclical (implying countercyclical industry concentration); 2) the market price and the industry average price-cost margin are both countercyclical; 3) the industry average marginal cost is countercyclical; and 4) the aggregate R&D spending is procyclical.

These patterns are driven by the two forces that are inherent in the Schumpeterian perspective on market competition. First, the changing structure of the industry resulting from the fluctuation in demand affects the severity of the selective pressure from market competition – i.e., the "selection effect." Second, the fluctuation in demand affects the intensity with which firms pursue their R&D, which determines the extent to which they are able to adapt to the changing technological environment – i.e., the "adaptation effect." The endogenous cyclical patterns observed in the time series can be understood in terms of the complex interactions between these two forces.

The computational model of industry dynamics developed here lends itself to further extensions. There are two important aspects of industry dynamics that are missing in the current version of the model but would be important to address. The first is the option for firms to merge with one another; the second is the role of patents in the Schumpeterian process of "creative destruction." These features are undoubtedly central to the current normative debates on the antitrust and technology policies. Although I have not taken the step into this territory in this book, I hope to have provided an appropriate foundation for further computational experiments that could allow normative policy analysis with respect to these important features.

The following perspective from Friedman (1953, p. 2) is apt: "Any policy conclusion necessarily rests on a prediction about the consequences of doing one thing rather than another, a prediction that must be based – implicitly or explicitly – on positive economics." The comparative statics approach in the tradition of the neoclassical equilibrium theory offers one way of generating such predictions. It is hoped that this book has demonstrated that the computational approach based on boundedly rational agents in a dynamic setting is another useful and effective approach to modeling behavior of firms and industries.

References

Armstrong, M. and Huck, S. (2010) "Behavioral economics as applied to firms: a primer," *Competition Policy International*, 6: 3–45.

Asplund, M. and Nocke, V. (2006) "Firm turnover in imperfectly competitive markets," *Review of Economic Studies*, 73: 295–327.

Axtell, R. and Epstein, J. M. (2006) "Coordination in transient social networks: an agent-based computational model of the timing of retirement," in J. M. Epstein (ed.), *Generative Social Science: Studies in Agent-based Computational Modeling*, Princeton, NJ: Princeton University Press.

Barlevy, G. (2007) "On the cyclicality of research and development," *American Economic Review*, 97: 1131–1164.

Bergstrom, T. C. and Varian, H. R. (1985) "When are Nash equilibria independent of the distribution of agents' characteristics?," *Review of Economic Studies*, 52: 715–718.

Bils, M. (1987) "The cyclical behavior of marginal cost and price," *American Economic Review*, 77: 838–855.

Boulding, K. E. (1970) *Economics as a Science*, New York: McGraw-Hill.

Bresnahan, T. F. and Reiss, P. C. (1991) "Entry and competition in concentrated markets," *Journal of Political Economy*, 99: 977–1009.

Burns, A. F. (1951) "Introduction," in W. C. Mitchell, *What Happens During Business Cycles: A Progress Report*, New York: National Bureau of Economic Research.

Byron, E. (2009) "P&G, Colgate hit by consumer thrift," *Wall Street Journal*, May 1: B1.

Camerer, C. and Ho, T.-H. (1999) "Experience-weighted attraction learning in normal form games," *Econometrica*, 67: 827–874.

Camerer, C. and Lovallo, D. (1999) "Overconfidence and excess entry: an experimental approach," *American Economic Review*, 89: 306–318.

Campbell, J. R. and Hopenhayn, H. A. (2005) "Market size matters," *Journal of Industrial Economics*, 53: 1–25.

Carroll, G. R. and Hannan, M. T. (2000) *The Demography of Corporations and Industries*, Princeton, NY: Princeton University Press.

Caves, R. E. (2007) "In praise of the old I.O.," *International Journal of Industrial Organization*, 25: 1–12.

Chang, M.-H. (2009) "Industry dynamics with knowledge-based competition: a computational study of entry and exit patterns," *Journal of Economic Interaction and Coordination*, 4: 73–114.

Chang, M.-H. (2011) "Entry, exit, and the endogenous market structure in technologically turbulent industries," *Eastern Economic Journal*, 37: 51–84.

Chang, M.-H. (forthcoming) "Computational industrial economics: a generative approach to dynamic analysis in industrial organization," in S.-H. Chen, M. Kaboudan, and Y.-R. Du (eds.), *Oxford Handbook on Computational Economics and Finance*, Oxford, UK: Oxford University Press.

Chatterjee, S., Cooper, R., and Ravikumar, B. (1993) "Strategic complementarity in business formation: aggregate fluctuations and sunspot equilibria," *Review of Economic Studies*, 60: 795–811.

Chevalier, J. A., Kashyap, A. K., and Rossi, P. E. (2003) "Why don't prices rise during periods of peak demand? Evidence from scanner data," *American Economic Review*, 93: 15–37.

Chevalier, J. A. and Scharfstein, D. S. (1996) "Capital-market imperfections and countercyclical markups: theory and evidence," *American Economic Review*, 86: 703–725.

Comin, D. and Gertler, M. (2006) "Medium-term business cycles," *American Economic Review*, 96: 523–551.

Cox, J. C. and Walker, M. (1998) "Learning to play Cournot duopoly strategies," *Journal of Economic Behavior & Organization*, 36: 141–161.

Dawid, H. (2006) "Agent-based models of innovation and technological change," in L. Tesfatsion and K. Judd (eds.), *Handbook of Computational Economics, Volume 2*, Amsterdam: Elsevier B.V.

Deissenberg, C., Van der Hoog, S., and Dawid, H. (2008) "EURACE: a massively parallel agent-based model of the European economy," *Applied Mathematics and Computation*, 204, 2: 541–552.

Devereux, M. B., Head, A. C., and Lapham, B. J. (1996) "Aggregate fluctuations with increasing returns to specialization and scale," *Journal of Economic Dynamics and Control*, 20: 627–656.

Doraszelski, U. and Pakes, A. (2007) "A framework for applied dynamic analysis in IO," in R. Schmalensee and R. D. Willig (eds.), *Handbook of Industrial Organization, Volume 2*, Amsterdam: Elsevier B.V.

Dosi, G. and Egidi, M. (1991) "Substantive and procedural uncertainty," *Journal of Evolutionary Economics*, 1: 145–168.

Dosi, G., Fagiolo, G., and Roventini, A. (2006) "An evolutionary model of endogenous business cycles," *Computational Economics*, 27: 3–34.

Dosi, G., Fagiolo, G., and Roventini, A. (2008) "The microfoundations of business cycles: an evolutionary, multi-agent model," *Journal of Evolutionary Economics*, 18: 413–432.

Dosi, G., Fagiolo, G., and Roventini, A. (2010) "Schumpeter meeting Keynes: a policy-friendly model of endogenous growth and business cycles," *Journal of Economics Dynamics and Control*, 34: 1748–1767.

Dunne, T., Roberts, M. J., and Samuelson, L. (1988) "Dynamic patterns of firm entry, exit, and growth," *RAND Journal of Economics*, 19: 495–515.

Epstein, J. M., Pankajakshan, R., and Hammond, R. A. (2011) "Combining computational fluid dynamics and agent-based modeling: a new approach to evacuation planning," *PloS one*, 6, 5: e20139.

Epstein, J. M., Cummings, D. A., Chakravarty, S., Singha, R. M., and Burke, D. S. (2006) "Toward a containment strategy for smallpox bioterror: an individual-based computational approach," in J. M. Epstein (ed.), *Generative Social Science: Studies in Agent-based Computational Modeling*, Princeton, NJ: Princeton University Press.

Ericson, R. and Pakes, A. (1995) "Markov-perfect industry dynamics: a framework for empirical work," *Review of Economic Studies*, 62: 53–82.

Etro, F. and Colciago, A. (2010) "Endogenous market structures and the business cycle," *Economic Journal*, 120: 1201–1233.

Fouraker, L. E. and Siegel, S. (1963) *Bargaining Behavior*, New York, NY: McGraw-Hill.

Friedman, M. (1953) *Essays in Positive Economics*, Chicago: The University of Chicago Press.

Geroski, P. A. (1995) "What do we know about entry?," *International Journal of Industrial Organization*, 13: 421–440.

Gort, M. and Klepper, S. (1982) "Time paths in the diffusion of product innovations," *Economic Journal*, 92: 630–653.

Green, E. J. and Porter, R. H. (1984) "Non-cooperative collusion under imperfect price information," *Econometrica*, 52: 87–100.

Haltiwanger, J. C. and Harrington Jr., J. E. (1991) "The impact of cyclical demand movements on collusive behavior," *RAND Journal of Economics*, 22: 89–106.

Hopenhayn, H. A. (1992) "Entry, exit, and firm dynamics in long run equilibrium," *Econometrica*, 60: 1127–1150.

Huck, S., Normann, H.-T., and Oechssler, J. (1999) "Learning in Cournot oligopoly: an experiment," *Economic Journal*, 109, C80–C95.

Jovanovic, B. (1982) "Selection and the evolution of industry," *Econometrica*, 50: 649–670.

Jovanovic, B. and MacDonald, G. M. (1994) "The life cycle of a competitive industry," *Journal of Political Economy*, 102: 322–347.

Kandori, M. (1991) "Correlated demand shocks and price wars during booms," *Review of Economic Studies*, 58: 171–180.

Kauffman, S. A. (1993) *The Origins of Order: Self-organization and Selection in Evolution*, Oxford, UK: Oxford University Press.

Kesmodel, D. (2009) "Beer makers plan more price boosts," *Wall Street Journal*, August 26: B1.

Klepper, S. (2002) "Firm survival and the evolution of oligopoly," *RAND Journal of Economics*, 33: 37–61.

Klepper, S. and Graddy, E. (1990) "The evolution of new industries and the determinants of market structure," *RAND Journal of Economics*, 21: 27–44.

Klepper, S. and Simons, K. L. (1997) "Technological extinctions of industrial firms: an inquiry into their nature and causes," *Industrial and Corporate Change*, 6: 379–460.

Klepper, S. and Simons, K. L. (2000a) "Dominance by birthright: entry of prior radio producers and competitive ramifications in the US television receiver industry," *Strategic Management Journal*, 21: 997–1016.

Klepper, S. and Simons, K. L. (2000b) "The making of an oligopoly: firm survival and technological change in the evolution of the US tire industry," *Journal of Political Economy*, 108: 728–760.

Knight, F. (1921) *Risk, Uncertainty and Profit*, Chicago: The University of Chicago Press.

Law, A. M. and Kelton, D. (2000) *Simulation Modeling and Analysis*, 3rd edition, New York, NY: McGraw-Hill.

Li, H., Sun, J., and Tesfatsion, L. (2011) "Testing institutional arrangements via agent-based modeling: a U.S. electricity market application," in H. Dawid and W. Semmler (eds.), *Computational Methods in Economic Dynamics*, Heidelberg, Germany: Springer.

MacDonald, J. M. (2000) "Demand, information, and competition: why do food prices fall at seasonal demand peaks?," *Journal of Industrial Economics*, 48: 27–45.

Mannaro, K., Marchesi, M., and Setzu, A. (2008) "Using an artificial financial market for assessing the impact of Tobin-like transaction taxes," *Journal of Economic Behavior and Organization*, 67: 445–462.

Marshall, A. (1920) *Principles of Economics*, 8th edition reprint 1968, New York, NY: The MacMillan Company.

Martins, J. O., Scarpetta, S., and Pilat, D. (1996) "Mark-up ratios in manufacturing industries: estimates for 14 OECD countries," *OECD Economics Department Working Papers*, No. 162.

Melitz, M. J. (2003) "The impact of trade on intra-industry reallocations and aggregate industry productivity," *Econometrica*, 71: 1695–1725.

Milgrom, P. and Roberts, J. (1990) "The economics of modern manufacturing: technology, strategy, and organization," *American Economic Review*, 511–528.

Nelson, R. R. and Winter, S. G. (1982) *An Evolutionary Theory of Economic Change*, Cambridge, MA: Harvard University Press.

Neugart, M. (2008) "Labor market policy evaluation with ACE," *Journal of Economic Behavior and Organization*, 67: 418–430.

Pakes, A. and Ericson, R. (1998) "Empirical implications of alternative models of firm dynamics," *Journal of Economic Theory*, 79, 1: 1–45.

Pakes, A. and McGuire, P. (1994) "Computing Markov-perfect Nash equilibria: numerical implications of a dynamic differentiated product model," *RAND Journal of Economics*, 25: 555–589.

Parker, J. and Epstein, J. M. (2011) "A distributed platform for global-scale agent-based models of disease transmission," *ACM Transactions on Modeling and Computer Simulation*, 22, 1: 2.

Porter, M. E. (1996) "What is strategy?," *Harvard Business Review*, 74: 61–78.

Rotemberg, J. J. and Saloner, G. (1986) "A supergame-theoretic model of price wars during booms," *American Economic Review*, 76: 390–407.

Rotemberg, J. J. and Woodford, M. (1990) "Cyclical markups: theories and evidence," *NBER*, No. 3534.

Rotemberg, J. J. and Woodford, M. (1999) "The cyclical behavior of prices and costs," in J. B. Taylor and M. Woodford (eds.), *Handbook of Macroeconomics, Volume 1*, Amsterdam: Elsevier B.V.

Russo, A., Catalano, M., Gallegati, M., Gaffeo, E., and Napoletano, M. (2007) "Industrial dynamics, fiscal policy and R&D: evidence from a computational experiment," *Journal of Economic Behavior and Organization*, 64: 426–447.

Schmalensee, R. (1989) "Inter-industry studies of structure and performance," in R. Schmalensee and R. D. Willig (eds.), *Handbook of Industrial Organization, Volume 2*, Amsterdam: Elsevier B.V.

Schumpeter, J. (1939) *Business Cycles: A Theoretical, Historical, and Statistical Analysis of the Capitalist Process*, New York, NY: McGraw-Hill.

Schumpeter, J. A. (1950) *Capitalism, Socialism, and Democracy*, 3rd edition, New York, NY: Harper.

Smith, P. H. (1968) *Wheels within Wheels: A Short History of American Motor Manufacturing*, New York, NY: Funk & Wagnalls.

Sun, J. and Tesfatsion, L. (2007) "Dynamic testing of wholesale power market designs: an open-source agent-based framework," *Computational Economics*, 30: 291–327.

Sutton, J. (1997) "Gibrat's legacy," *Journal of Economic Literature*, 35: 40–59.

Tesfatsion, L. and Judd, K. (eds.) (2006) *Handbook of Computational Economics, Volume 2: Agent-Based Computational Economics*, Amsterdam: Elsevier B.V.

Theocharis, R. (1960) "On the stability of the Cournot solution on the oligopoly problem," *Review of Economic Studies*, 27: 133–134.

Thompson, D. (1917) *On Growth and Form*, Cambridge, UK: Cambridge University Press.

Warner, E. J. and Barsky, R. B. (1995) "The timing and magnitude of retail store markdowns: evidence from weekends and holidays," *Quarterly Journal of Economics*, 110: 321–352.

Weintraub, G., Benkard, L., and Van Roy, B. (2008) "Markov perfect industry dynamics with many firms," *Econometrica*, 76: 1375–1411.

Weintraub, G., Benkard, L., and Van Roy, B. (2010) "Computational methods for oblivious equilibrium," *Operations Research*, 58: 1247–1265.

Weiss, L. W. (1989) *Concentration and Price*, Cambridge, MA: The MIT Press.

Westerhoff, F. and Dieci, R. (2008) "The use of agent-based financial market models to test the effectiveness of regulatory policies," *Journal of Economics and Statistics*, 228, 2/3: 195–227.

Index

ACE *see* agent-based computational economics
adaptation effect 118, 119
agent-based computational economics 12, 13
AMES model 15
Asplund, M. 10

backward-looking behavior 4
between-industry variations 84
bounded rationality 3, 4

Camerer, C. 32, 38
Caves, R. E. 95
Chang, M.-H. 34, 35
Cournot-Nash equilibrium 27
creative destruction 131
cross-industries studies 95
curse of dimensionality 12
cyclical industrial dynamics 115

Dawid, H. 14
deterministic variation in demand 123
Doraszelski, U. 12
Dunne, T. 2, 76

Ericson, R. 12
Experience-Weighted Attraction (EWA) learning 38

Friedman, M. 134

Geroski, P. A. 79, 81
Gini coefficient 45
Gort, M. 55

Graddy, E. 2, 55, 57

Hamming distance 20, 23
Herfindahl-Hirschmann Index 45
Ho, T.-H. 38
Hopenhayn, H. A. 10

imitation 36
imitative R&D 22
industry marginal cost 46
infant mortality 55, 106, 110
innovation 36
innovative R&D 22
inter-industry volatility 85
intra-industry volatility 85

Jovanovic, B. 9, 55, 57
Judd, K. 12

Kauffman, S. A. 40
Klepper, S. 2, 55, 57

life span of firms 106
Lovallo, D. 32

MacDonald, G. M. 55, 57
McGuire, P. 12
market share inequality 104–106
Markov perfect equilibrium models 11
Milgrom, P. 18
myopia 2, 3

Nelson, R. R. 13, 131
NK-model 40

Nocke, V. 10
non-equilibrium dynamics 1

optimal technology 23

Pakes, A. 12
Porter, M. E. 18
power law 108
price-cost margins 46

recurrent shakeouts 71, 81
Roberts, J. 18
Roberts, M. J. 2, 76
"roulette wheel" algorithm 37

Samuelson, L. 2, 76
Schmalensee, R. 95
Schumpeter, J. 17, 99
Schumpeterian competition 17, 131, 132

selection effect 118, 119
shakeouts 54
Smith, P. H. 54–55, 56, 75
"start-up" wealth 31
static free-entry equilibrium 27
stationary equilibrium models 10
steady state 6, 77
stochastic variation in demand 120
system of activities 18, 40

tasks 19
technological diversity 45, 99–103
Tesfatsion, L. 12, 15

US automobile industry 54, 56, 107, 108
US automobile tire industry 58, 59

Winter, S. G. 13, 131

eBooks
from Taylor & Francis

Helping you to choose the right eBooks for your Library

Add to your library's digital collection today with Taylor & Francis eBooks. We have over 50,000 eBooks in the Humanities, Social Sciences, Behavioural Sciences, Built Environment and Law, from leading imprints, including Routledge, Focal Press and Psychology Press.

ORDER YOUR FREE INSTITUTIONAL TRIAL TODAY

Free Trials Available

We offer free trials to qualifying academic, corporate and government customers.

Choose from a range of subject packages or create your own!

Benefits for you

- ■ Free MARC records
- ■ COUNTER-compliant usage statistics
- ■ Flexible purchase and pricing options
- ■ 70% approx of our eBooks are now DRM-free.

Benefits for your user

- ■ Off-site, anytime access via Athens or referring URL
- ■ Print or copy pages or chapters
- ■ Full content search
- ■ Bookmark, highlight and annotate text
- ■ Access to thousands of pages of quality research at the click of a button.

eCollections

Choose from 20 different subject eCollections, including:

Asian Studies

Economics

Health Studies

Law

Middle East Studies

eFocus

We have 16 cutting-edge interdisciplinary collections, including:

Development Studies

The Environment

Islam

Korea

Urban Studies

For more information, pricing enquiries or to order a free trial, please contact your local sales team:

UK/Rest of World: **online.sales@tandf.co.uk**
USA/Canada/Latin America: **e-reference@taylorandfrancis.com**
East/Southeast Asia: **martin.jack@tandf.com.sg**
India: **journalsales@tandfindia.com**

■ **www.tandfebooks.com** ■■■■■■■■■■ ■■■■ ■ ■■■■■

Printed in the United States
by Baker & Taylor Publisher Services